W9-ACP-803

The Poems of TIBULLUS

INDIANA UNIVERSITY GREEK AND LATIN CLASSICS

OVID'S METAMORPHOSES translated by Rolfe Humphries

OVID'S THE ART OF LOVE translated by Rolfe Humphries

THE SATIRES OF JUVENAL translated by Rolfe Humphries

LUCIAN'S TRUE HISTORY or LUCIUS AND THE ASS translated by Paul Turner

THREE GREEK PLAYS FOR THE THEATRE
(MEDEA, CYCLOPS, THE FROGS) translated by Peter D. Arnott

THE SATIRES OF PERSIUS translated by W. S. Merwin

THE HISTORIES OF POLYBIUS translated by Evelyn S. Shuckburgh

THE GOLDEN ASS BY APULEIUS translated by Jack Lindsay

VERGIL'S AENEID translated by L. R. Lind

SELECTED EPIGRAMS OF MARTIAL translated by Rolfe Humphries

THE POEMS OF PROPERTIUS translated by Constance Carrier

SENECA: HIS TENNE TRAGEDIES
collected by Thomas Newton, introduction by T. S. Eliot

THE TROJAN WAR: *The Chronicles of Dictys of Crete and Dares the Phrygian*
translated by R. M. Frazer, Jr.

GREEK LYRIC POETRY translated by Willis Barnstone

THE POEMS OF

TIBULLUS

translated by Constance Carrier

with introduction, notes, and glossary

by Edward M. Michael

INDIANA UNIVERSITY PRESS

BLOOMINGTON & LONDON

Library of Congress catalog card number: 68-14614
Manufactured in the United States of America

CONTENTS

INTRODUCTION

TIBULLUS wrote elegies, but not in the modern sense of the word. For us an "elegy" implies a sad and meditative poem written in a country church-yard. The mood defines the poetic form. But in ancient Greece and Rome "elegy" was defined only by its metrical form—a series of alternating dactylic hexameters and pentameters. Its themes and moods could vary. It is hardly necessary to attempt here to trace systematically the development of this literary genre. It should be pointed out, however, that in Greece it was not always limited, as it tends to be in the Roman treatment, to the realm of love. True, the early Greek elegists, noticeably Mimnermus, did occasionally select love as their basic theme. But in addition the form could serve to communicate a variety of themes and moods. It could be used to express patriotic feeling, or it could take the form of a lamentation. It could be didactic or merely descriptive. But it was forever a personal kind of poetry.

To be sure, all poetry must be contemplative. But this is especially true of elegy. Regardless of the immediate theme or mood, emotional response—the shock value—always results through the personal reflection of the poet and reader. Curiously enough, the very meter assists in bringing this about: rhythmically, the two lines of an elegiac couplet have different tenors. The long hexameter readily lends itself to a narrative-descriptive aspect, while the somewhat shorter pentameter, with its halting caesura at the middle of the line, is ideally suited to a reflective-contemplative aspect. The two lines reinforce each other and together produce a most appropriate rhythmical frame for this type of poetry.

Cast into this frame, Greek elegy gradually took on a sentimental and erotic mood. For our purposes, its romanticized development during the Alexandrian era is particularly noteworthy. Although relatively few elegies have survived from this period, we know pretty well what the form was like. In an age of extreme erudition, elegy too became erudite and formal, with the emphasis on stylistics. Poets vied with each other to see who could be more obscure in his allusions, more complicated in his structure, and more recondite in his use of language. Arcadian commonplaces abound, together with a general excess of antiquarianism. In short, form became most important.

Although elegy is a major vehicle for Latin amorous expression, for many years it was relatively neglected by classical scholars, to say nothing of the general reading public. Perhaps the chief reason for this stems from the common but somewhat misleading notion that the bulk of Latin literature is not original. It is, we are told, modeled after Greek sources. In the case of the Roman elegists, no one will deny the influence of their Greek predecessors. But the degree and true nature of literary influence is a touchy matter. Although Roman elegy does demonstrably share many of the salient characteristics of its Greek sources, these unfortunately have been stressed to such an extent that the Roman element of originality more often than not has been overlooked, or, if observed at all, grossly misunderstood.

The Romans themselves, far more cognizant of Greek literary tradition than we can ever be, realized that elegy written in Latin need not be considered inferior to elegy written in Greek. Quintilian, writing at the end of the first century A.D., states in his *Handbook of Rhetoric:*

> In the genre of Elegy also we
> compete with the Greeks.
> *Inst. Orat.* 10.1.93

This is true because there is something inevitably "Roman" about the Roman elegists (no tautological statement this), even when they are seemingly most influenced by their Greek forerunners. It was a form which the Romans borrowed. But the specific handling of it, the contents placed within its bounds, and the resultant poetic merit is Roman—and quite original. Classicists, having come to recognize this fact, have rescued Roman elegy from its state of relative neglect, and concomitant with their renewed interest is the gradual availability in English of the works of these Roman poets of love.

Poets have usually been very reluctant to talk about their poetry. They are only a little more likely to talk about themselves. In the case of Tibullus, we can glean occasional biographical snippets in his elegies, but these are offered incidentally within a larger scope and consequently do not give us many detailed particulars. Of somewhat more importance are two texts which are appended to some of the manuscripts. The first, an anonymous *Life (vita Tibulli)* does fill in some of the gaps, but it is of questionable authority, since it is clearly a very late addition.[1] The other is an epigram, apparently fragmentary, which is usually ascribed to the Augustan poet Domitius Marsus, little of whose work has survived. Beyond this we must rely upon the periodic references to Tibullus found in other Latin writers.

The year of Tibullus' death can be fixed with relative certainty at 19 B.C., for it is the very point of Domitius' epigram that our poet's death followed very closely that of Vergil. As for the year of his birth, we simply do not know. We do know that at the time of his death Tibullus was young.[2] Horace (born 65 B.C.) speaks of him as a younger man.[3] These clues, coupled with additional testimony of Ovid in which he lists the Roman elegists chronologically,[4] would lead us to believe that the period between 55 and 50 B.C. is a safe estimate. And so, like Catullus, Tibullus died before his time.

Tibullus' praenomen has not survived, and this is indicative of the shadowy state of his biography. He is known to us as Albius Tibullus. Unlike many of his contemporary literary figures, he was born of old Latin stock in Latium, not far from Rome. The probable location, Horace tells us,[5] was near Pedum, which lay near the Sabine Hills between Tibur and Praeneste. He goes on to remark that Tibullus was never a "body without soul" and that the gods had given him good looks and riches along with the art of enjoying them. Specifically, the Albii belonged to the equestrian order, and it was probably on his ancestral estate that Tibullus was born. He certainly spent his adolescence there and does not seem to have spent extended periods of time away from home. As we shall see, one of the main motives in Tibullus' poetry is his love of country life. Undoubtedly the rural setting of his boyhood years played a significant part in fostering this taste.

Somehow he became associated with Marcus Valerius Messalla Corvinus (64 B.C.-8 A.D.), the statesman, orator, and, along with Maecenas, great patron of literature in the Augustan Age. We can only conjecture as to the immediate circumstance of the introduction. Messalla himself came from an aristocratic family and was conservative in his politics, at least early in his career. It has been suggested that, given the socio-economic background of the Albian family and its corollary conservative predilections, the introduction came about through mutual friends. Perhaps the trigger for the introduction was the fact that Tibullus, like Vergil, Propertius, and others, suffered from the land confiscations which took place after the Battle of Philippi (42 B.C.). But this is of secondary importance. One thing is certain: Messalla recognized in Tibullus a kindred spirit and a talent worthy of his patronage.

The poet accompanied and served his new-found friend on various military campaigns. And apparently he served well, for in commemorating Messalla's victory over the Aquitanians in 27 B.C., Tibullus could remark:

> Not without me was that glory won where the Pyrenees
> beyond the harbor town rise dark and tall.
>
> I.vii.9f., trans. Constance Carrier

But military service did not suit Tibullus' temperament. He terminated forever this type of activity in order to serve in the special camp that he had chosen. He is a writer of elegies, and his camp is that of love.

Whereas the erotic lyrics of Horace are concerned with many women, it seems to have been a convention of Roman elegy that the poet have only one woman as the prime heroine of his verse. It is she who causes the poet's joy, or grief, as the case may be. This tradition undoubtedly goes back to Mimnermus' collection of elegies centered around his love, Nanno. Catullus, the first Roman to experiment successfully with elegy, had his Lesbia. Of the elegists proper, Propertius had his Cynthia, and Ovid his Corinna. Tibullus had not one, but two women who figure in his love life. It is no less true of Tibullus than it is of his fellow love-poets that a proper evaluation of his poetry must in part proceed from an understanding of his love relationships. Such an understanding does not come readily, for the phenomenon of love is always an ever-renewing, unique experience. Hence, the critic of love poetry must, *pace* the poets, pry to a certain extent.

According to common Roman poetic practice the first poem in any collection is particularly noteworthy. It is usually the *last* poem written in chronological sequence. As a result its character cannot help but be at least partially determined by the poet's awareness of the subject matter of the rest of the poems in his collection. Usually the first poem is dedicated either to the poet's patron or to some other close friend. Hence the entire collection is dedicated in his honor. It does not surprise us, then, that Messalla Corvinus is the recipient of Tibullus' first book, published about 26 B.C. But we should notice that he is addressed only after the first poem is well under way, and not in the direct, flattering manner, say, that Horace extols Maecenas (his literary patron) at the very beginning of the first book of *Odes*. The reference to Messalla enters in primarily because it is part of the poem's structure, and not because it might increase the poet's allowance. Tibullus is above all else sincere.

In addition to being dedicatory, the first poem in a collection is often synoptical. The poem as a whole can serve as a basic statement of the poet's situation—anticipatory of the elaboration to follow in the other poems. In other words, we have a snapshot which sets the scene for the moving picture. Thus, we find a protactic function in Tibullus' opening elegy. Although this is a love poem, there is little mention of love until line 45, and Delia,[6] Tibullus' first love, is not mentioned until toward the end of the poem. What precedes is as essential for Tibullus and our proper understanding of his poetry as it has been enigmatic for some critics. For prior to the love motive, the poet covers most of the other motives which will be found in the rest of his poetry. And it is this very multiplicity of themes and their treatment which accounts to a great extent for Tibullus' lack of popularity in the past. He and his poetry have actually been described as "anaemic." But, as we shall see, this judgment is unwarranted.

Let us look closely at the various themes in the first poem. The basic substance of the long passage before the love motive is Tibullus' deep-rooted affection for country life. We all find pleasure in the serenity of a rural setting, but for Tibullus the country is more than a source of pleasure; it is a nourishing need. The poem begins with the motive of the poet's *paupertas*. We hear for the first time a statement which will be recurrent: Tibullus has no need for riches. To live in poverty[7] in a country environment is all that he desires, and the basic premise for his part in such a world proceeds from the wish:

> If I may move in peace, poor in all but contentment.
>
> I.i.7, trans. Constance Carrier

For Tibullus peace is not possible unless there is total separation from war. Appropriately, the motif of the poet's abhorrence of war is anticipated within the initial reference to his poverty, for it is out of greed for riches that men wage wars. Tibullus goes on to describe the various aspects of country life from which he derives contentment. We have almost a catalogue of chores. He presents these aspects in a dream world in which he tries to capture happiness as it was in the Golden Age. Within his reverie it does not surprise us that the poet makes frequent reference to native rustic divinities and to country superstitions. We have, then, still another motif which borders on the supernatural. Further, since it is a primitive age for which Tibullus longs, his allusions themselves are often examples of primitivism:

> Gods, be with me; accept gifts from my humble table
> poured into earthen cups, set on a scoured board.
> Such were the cups the first countryman made to drink from,
> shaping them with his hands out of the pliant clay.
>
> I.i.37ff., trans. Constance Carrier

But Tibullus' dream world is soon disturbed by his recognition of reality. In typical Tibullan fashion we have a sudden contrast between the past and present. The truth is that men do seek riches, they fight wars, and they enjoy the glory which they derive from their conquests. Here, Messalla is mentioned as one whose temperament is suited to such glory. But immediately, again through sudden contrast, Tibullus disavows such a life and gives us the source of *his* glory:

> Delia, my dear delight, you are the glory I yearn for.
> "Wastrel"—I welcome the slur, spending my life in love.
> Yours is the face I would see, my last hour upon me;
> yours is the hand I would hold, talisman and touchstone;
> yours the tears that would almost quench the flames
> at my bier.
> Tears and kisses together, mingled bitter and tender!
>
> I.i.57ff., trans. Constance Carrier

But notice that the poet expresses his love for Delia within a mood of gloom. He talks of his inevitable death and the grief which it will cause his love. He continues much in the same vein:

> Meanwhile O come close! Love, make us one in living;
> dark-hooded death will come all too soon to part us,
> all too soon we'll grow old; Love will find us grotesque,
> then,
> palsied and white-headed, mouthing the speech of Love.
> I.i.69ff., trans. Constance Carrier

It is at this point that Tibullus comes to an awareness of his own reality within the context of the reality of a world in which he is forced to live. How will he proceed? He will cast aside the gloom, and with almost a *carpe diem* outlook, will experience consummate joy:

> Now is our day, our night—shameless, I'll break
> down doors,
> out of sheer joy in life stir up a lively brawl.
> I.i.73f., trans. Constance Carrier

The poem ends, through the device of ring-composition, with still another reference to the poet's *paupertas* and contentment.

Do not look for impassioned pleas in this poem; you will not find them. There is, however, the compelling aura of a love experience that is very profound. It *cannot* be characterized by passion. This is not to say that Tibullus was passionless. But we do sense in our poet a *soft* fire which burns quietly, and it is this particular manifestation of love which Tibullus so often connects with his borrowed dream of the idealized past which knew no conflicts. A passage from another poem will show more clearly how this connection is made:

> "A little house, and Delia watching over
> grain on the threshing floor in sunlit dust,
> or over grapes, piled till the troughs are brimming
> and the quick feet tread out the fragrant must.

> She'll learn to count the flocks; the servants' baby
> she'll teach, and talk to it, and dry its tears;
> she'll give the harvest gods, for vines, a cluster,
> for flocks, drink-offering, for corn, spiked ears.
> Heart of the house, she'll love its things, its people,
> while I—being nothing, I shall be at ease."
>
> I.v.21ff., trans. Constance Carrier

Obviously, Tibullus could love Delia and the country separately for themselves. But how much more intensified and gratifying is his amorous love when it has as its setting the relative loneliness of the country. Here Tibullus can be totally captivated and released from any potential anxiety. It is the very happiness which he derives from love in such a setting which serves to give him protection and security:

> Who would not envy me, holding my love in my arms,
> warm in the winter night, hearing the wild winds rage—
> or, when the cold South wind blows and the rain hisses,
> both of us sound asleep, lulled by the storm's wailing.
>
> I.i.45ff., trans. Constance Carrier

Call Tibullus an escapist if you will. His escape, however, is always natural and facile. There is nothing artificial in the poet's desire for country life. He is sincerely devoted to it. Nor is there really anything artificial about the poet's depiction of such a life. True, it looms forever hazy for the modern reader. But, again, this is because of the degree of Tibullus' sincerity. He does not paint his rustic setting in the way that Theocritus does in his *Idylls*, or Vergil in the *Eclogues*. They construct their pastoral settings around specific characters and tangible events. Theirs is a world of shepherds involved in particular circumstances. They follow the Alexandrian tradition and one questions their sincerity in writing. As for Horace, his pastoral landscape is a place in which he himself actually lives and is involved. But his depiction tends to be academic. Tibullus' Arcady, on the other hand, is constructed not as a place but as a mood, and it is his intentional haziness which serves to delineate that mood. In other words, he attempts to describe not setting so much as his personal dependence upon and emotional reaction to a chosen way of life. His ideal world may not be one in which he actually lives—try as he may—but it is the only one in which he could be truly happy. This same underlying sincerity is to be found in Tibullus' love relationship. As a result, in order to express his love for Delia, the poet may seem to be unassertive. But the point is that he need not take recourse to the graphics of Catullus or Propertius. His sincerity is justification enough for his love.

We can now more clearly define the nature of Tibullus' amorous love. It has been pointed out that our poet expresses this love partially within a mood of gloom—we cannot help but sense the threatening presence of death. Indeed, we frequently sense Tibullus' awareness of the fleeting moment itself. But it would be wrong to say that he desires to escape from a fear of death or of growing old. It is the accomplishment of our poet that he succeeded in subordinating these fears, common to all, to his love for Delia. His death will be dreadful if it happens far away from Delia, if she is not present to cry and participate in his burial. But when she is close, preferably in the country, death itself will be beautiful. We have also noticed Tibullus' distaste for ambitious public life and the glory and riches derived from it. Again, Tibullus is sincere in his scorn of riches. He does not so much desire to escape from the reality of the world about him as to abandon himself to infinitely greater needs—love and country life. And these constitute the circle around which Tibullus' poetry moves. In effect, our poet resigns his entire being to these two needs alone. Country life is not the setting for Tibullus' poetry. It is, however, one of his basic concerns. It reflects the very desire of the poet's soul, which longs to find some degree of peace under circumstances when consolation can be found only in resignation to everything—yes, to death itself. Here, then, is a basic characteristic of Tibullus: his complete abandonment to country life and to another human being who can take and offer love. The poet immerses this abandonment in the realm of the idealized past, for it was then that true contentment could be known. The two motives, then—love for country life and love for Delia—stemming from the selfsame sincerity, reinforce each other, and it is the poet's dependence upon both of them which gives them a special unity, even when they are treated separately.

Unfortunately, Tibullus did not live to ripe old age with Delia at his side. In the second poem of Book I the poet laments that Delia is separated from him. He must now contend with that convention of erotic poetry, the rival—the "rich lover" (*dives amator*). Tibullus describes his situation within the poetic form of the paraclausithyron, or lament of the "shut-out lover" (*exclusus amator*) before the door which stands closed between lover and loved one. Although Delia obviously left Tibullus of her own choosing, the poet imagines that she is "jailed," forcibly kept from him. His one desire is to free his love from captivity and to trick the rival. Hence:

> Rain, lash the door of that stone-hearted guardian!
> Jove, aim your thunder at that bolted door!
> Door, hear my plaint and open to me only;
> in stealth, in silence, let me enter in.
> If I have spoken ill of you, or cursed you,
> let it be on my own head now, that sin.
> Think of the phrases I've rehearsed before you,
> the flowers I've brought to make your threshold gay.
> Keep up your courage, Delia; trick your jailer—
> Love laughs at locksmiths, so the wise men say.
>
> I.ii.7ff., trans. Constance Carrier

Notice that the address begins almost as a tirade, but quickly takes the form of a supplication, clearly aimed at gaining entrée to Delia. This and the reference to gifts placed before the door are usual in this poetic form. Also characteristic is the poet's willingness to put up with any hardships, as long as he can have access once again to his love:

I walk through winter nights and scarcely shiver,
the cold rain soaks me and I do not care.
And what would cure me now? My Delia's finger
at the opened gate, to summon me inside.
I.ii.29., trans. Constance Carrier

To aid in this recovery Tibullus enlists the help of a witch. There enters in, then, the motive of the supernatural, an indication of the poet's desperation. But witchcraft does not help. The thought occurs to the poet that he himself is to blame for unwittingly having slighted Venus. Again, desperate man that he is, he is willing to pay the necessary penalty, as long as a resolution comes about. As abject suppliant he ends the poem:

Be gentle, Venus. Hear the songs I sing,
nor, angered, burn the offerings I bring.
I.ii.97f. trans. Constance Carrier

But in the face of reality how does Tibullus act?

More wine, more wine, to wash away new troubles,
to let sleep triumph and my eyelids close;
and when I lie there, my flushed temples throbbing,
do not break in on that ill-starred repose.
I.ii.1ff., trans. Constance Carrier

Although Tibullus borrows the conventional form of the paraclausithyron, his treatment of it shows marked originality. The actual address to the door covers relatively few lines (7-14). To be sure, there are references to the door aside from this passage, and the poet manages to cover many of the traditional formulae which are characteristic of the poetic form. But Tibullus does not write his paraclausithyron as a literary exercise. The borrowed form is merely the immediate setting for the communication of something uniquely personal and pathetic—Tibullus' emotional state. He has a certain confidence in winning Delia back, but he expresses it through a pitiable fantasy which is almost convincing until we realize that it is merely a manifestation of the poet's depressed confusion in face of a reality which he cannot justify. Tibullus has resigned himself to one love, but he has not learned that lover does not own loved one. Various Tibullan motives appear within the poem's structure, and admittedly there is some degree of rambling. But it is of a superficial sort. We must be careful not to insist that poets be logical—love poets more frequently are not! The motives are there because they are part of Tibullus' world of resignation. If there seems to be structural rambling, it is because Tibullus' current state of mind does not conform to logical thought patterns.

Similarly, the poet borrows the form of the propemptikon (bon voyage poem) for the next poem, but adjusts it to serve special purposes. Tibullus had accompanied Messalla on an eastward campaign, but because of illness at Corcyra, could not continue. And so, bon voyage to Messalla, who must proceed without his friend! But it is the theme of love which occupies the second half of the poem. Taking advantage of his illness, Tibullus again dwells upon his possible death far away from Delia. The spatial separation raises certain doubts in the poet's mind, and in the last lines he tries to overcome his suspicions of an unfaithful Delia, thus removed, by resorting once again to fantasy:

> Delia, I beg of you, stay true to me in my absence;
> give gossip no chance to start; keep your maidservant near;
> hear the stories she tells in the quiet lamp-lit evenings
> while she holds the distaff, spinning the long thread,
> and all around her the others bend to the tasks you have set them,
> till sleep comes touching gently mistress as well as maid—
> O then let me be at the door, sudden and unreported,
> so that it seems to you I have dropped from the sky,
> and O come running out to meet me, breathless and barefoot,
> your bright hair blown like a flag—O Delia, welcome me!
> This is my only prayer: star in the brightening blue,
> Dawn, driving your rosy horses, O make it true!
>
> I.iii.83ff., trans. Constance Carrier

Since it was Messalla's campaign that separated Tibullus from Delia, it does not surprise us that a large portion of this poem is concerned with the antithesis of war and peace. But the poem's unity does not suffer, for this very motive serves to heighten the poet's loneliness. It gives us in itself a contrast between Tibullus' actual situation and his dream world. In form the poem is a propemptikon. But Tibullus' emotional state is so graphically sketched that at the poem's end the modern reader excitedly hopes along with the poet that his wish will come true.

The fact remains that Tibullus did lose Delia. We have seen that he took consolation in wine in face of the failing love affair. He may also have resorted to the paraphiliac expedient of homosexual love. For in the fourth poem of the first book our poet writes of his love for the boy Marathus, and he receives instruction in specific amorous procedures from Priapus himself. This poem is usually viewed as a *tour de force*, an example of the *paignion*, or trifling, playful composition so dear to the Alexandrians. It is true that in the following two poems Tibullus seemingly assures Delia that the Marathus poem was simply a literary exercise. Still, our poet writes about the boy in other poems in this book (nos. 8 and 9), and it is questionable whether they are as frivolous and artificial as some critics would think. In apologizing for the first Marathus poem, Tibullus may have simply attempted to swallow his pride.

It is not necessary to trace the history of the Delia affair beyond this point. Let it suffice to say that Delia becomes increasingly remote. She is gradually transformed into a common prostitute who desires only banal gifts from her rich lover. Tibullus becomes increasingly aware of this reality, and his final attempts to regain her, made through self-delusion, fail. Perhaps Delia was only the beautiful reflection of Tibullus' youthful desires. Perhaps he wanted someone around him like Venus as he conceived her, a love so sincere that it could inspire universal love. But such a love toppled from its pedestal, and the poet proceeded to find oblivion in wine—and perhaps in Marathus. And when this became impossible, he turned to another woman, Nemesis, and it is with her that the love elegies of Book II are concerned.

The erotic mood of this book, perhaps published posthumously, is completely different from that of the first book. The very name Nemesis, undoubtedly a pseudonym, typifies Tibullus' desire to get even with Delia, to achieve some degree of retaliation for the injuries which he suffered at her hands. Curiously enough, Nemesis has much in common with the transformed Delia. She is a prostitute, and her favors are offered at a fixed price. Those who cannot pay waste her time. And so, the logic which runs through Tibullus' mind is something like this: "If this be love, Delia, then I shall become an expert in it." And it was through Nemesis that the poet would gain his expertise. Generally, we detect little of the sincere warmth which was so characteristic of the first love relationship. On the contrary, the poet, knowing what Nemesis is and her brand of love, yet slave to the passion which she kindles, states in cold realism:

> She waits, and with her, bondage;
> my fathers' freedom, farewell!
> Slavery, chains, are my fate now,
> the tight-bound shackles of love
> to chafe me, all too unjustly
> My cruel girl holds the torch
> to my flesh—I would turn to stone
> on the cold hills to escape,
> or turn to a wind-vexed cliff
> for waves to hurl ships against.
> Bleak days and bleaker nights,
> no moment without new gall;
> no help in song, or its god—
> her hand is outstretched for gold.
> II.iv.1ff., trans. Constance Carrier

Quiet, sincere, resigned love, then, has seemingly evolved into passion. Love as Tibullus originally conceived it did not succeed for him. With this new brand the poet realized, I suspect, how ugly love can in fact be, forcing the lover to commit sacrilege:

> Must I murder and steal for gifts
> to pass that wept-at gate?
> must I rob the holy shrines?
> Love's temple shall be the first,
> for he prompts me thus, and makes
> my mistress grasping. His, first!
>
> II.iv.21ff., trans. Constance Carrier

Here and elsewhere in the second book Tibullus could wish that he were rich so as to win the love of the fickle and selfish woman who tortures him. The tragedy of the situation is that it is a wholly unworthy object that inspires the poet's degrading passion. But passion it seems to be, and desperate Tibullus is graphic in describing it:

> Medea's brew, and Circe's,
> all the Thessalian herbs,
> even the slimy fluid
> a mare gives off in heat—
> all these let Nemesis mix
> in my drink, and if she smiles
> I swear I will swallow it down.
>
> II.iv.55ff., trans. Constance Carrier

The crucial question that we must ask is whether Tibullus believed that Nemesis, regardless of what she was, could somehow fulfill his desideratum. Or, as a result of his disillusioning affair with Delia, did the poet give up all hope of finding true love? Is he a used-up man who has lost all of his fight? Is he content to satisfy his animal instincts only? It is tempting to answer yes to these questions, until we realize that the poet simply is not convincing when he writes of his love for Nemesis as sheer passion alone. In fact, by his stressing the sensual to such a degree we sense that Tibullus constructs illusions around the woman and that these again are manifestations of his loneliness which serve to mask what is still a prevalent need and hope for love:

> I would have killed myself long since, but Hope
> tempts me, and I believe her promises.
> Why does she keep that spark alive in men?
>
> II.vi.19ff., trans. Constance Carrier

It might be argued that Tibullus hopes merely for access to the physical Nemesis who is temporarily not available. But this, the sixth poem of Book II, is not a poem of passion; it is a poem of love tragedy. In a highly wrought passage of personal intensity Tibullus begs that Nemesis soften for the sake of her sister who recently died. The latter will intercede for Tibullus, and Nemesis must not anger her spirit by refusing to be merciful to the poet. Tibullus' rehearsal of the tragic death of the girl might cause renewed grief for Nemesis. Hence, Tibullus drops the subject, and the poem ends on a note of paranoia that is very much like mental pain:

> I'll say no more; I would not renew your tears:
> I am not worth one cry of pain from you.
> Sorrow should never redden those eloquent eyes.
> You are good. It is Phryne, Phryne the bawd, that I fear.
> With hidden poisons I know she plots my death;
> though I hear your voice beyond the door, she'll say,
> the liar, that no, her mistress is not at home;
> or when I come to spend a promised night,
> she'll swear that you're ill, or that the omens are wrong.
> Then I could die, indeed, and, desperate,
> ask myself whose arms are holding you.
> Damn you, Phryne—your life should be hard to bear
> if the gods heed half of what I say of you.
>
> II.vi.41ff., trans. Constance Carrier

What Tibullus really hopes for is the true love which Nemesis by definition cannot give. The poet himself has not changed much. Perhaps the possibilities of finding such love may have become increasingly remote, but he has not given up the hope that it will someday, somehow be found—even in a girl like Nemesis. With the failure of his first love, Tibullus did not, like some men, lose his capacity to love. On the contrary, I suspect that it was intensified—but under circumstances which were anything but encouraging. Thus, although Tibullus creates illusions, we see through them into his mind, which knows too well that man was not meant to remain alone. It is his very fear of being alone and his constant searching, frustrated by his inability to find his own image in the world, which are the basic characteristics of our poet's originality. Behind the fantasies and delusions there remains the lonely and sincere Tibullus.

And yet, not all of Tibullus' poems treat of the love theme exclusively. Apparently the genethliacon, or "happy birthday" poem, was a favorite form of composition in Messalla's literary circle, and Tibullus gives us two examples. The seventh poem of Book I was written on the occasion of Messalla's birthday. But it serves a double purpose in that it also congratulates Messalla for his victory over the Aquitanians. And so the poem has in part an historical context. But Tibullus weaves this context into an imaginative and vivid depiction of the various landscapes in which he served his friend in past times, and it is this successful blending of the two themes which sets off his treatment of this form. Again, our poet shows originality in celebrating the birthday of Cornutus, another friend, in the second poem of Book II. Tibullus actually vivifies Cornutus' "guardian angel" and anticipates his friend's birthday wish. But more than this, Tibullus himself interprets the final will of the angel whom we see so vividly in our presence.

The tenth poem of the first book is a diatribe on war which admittedly does employ many stock conceits. But over them there predominates the poet's highly personal and sincere reflections, which are frequently cast within primitivistic allusions. And it is this special coloring which serves to make Tibullus' prayer for peace all the more universally applicable.

In the opening poem of Book II Tibullus celebrates the *Ambarvalia*, a native rural festival. There is a marked religious aura, especepecially when our poet gives us the specific details of the ritual. But Tibullus uses the festival only as a starting point from which to praise the rustic life in general. He has, of course, done this before. But the country life pictured in this poem is far more tangible. There is a certain note of immediacy. We do not feel that Tibullus writes in a reverie; rather the festival comes alive for us and we can imagine it taking place yearly in every Italian village. Even though the poem is Alexandrian in style, its subject matter is clearly Roman, and its vividness testifies to Tibullus' graphic skill.

Tibullus' longest poem is the fifth in Book II. It is also unique in that it is his only poem of a national character. It was written to commemorate the election of M. Valerius Messallinus, Messalla's eldest son, to the board of Quindecemviri. But this only occasioned the poem's composition. Its real subject matter consists of various topics which range from the legend of Aeneas and the founding of Rome to Augustus' victory over Antony and Cleopatra. It is a poem in praise of Rome. But again the descriptions are so graphically constructed that one soon realizes that the national propaganda almost loses itself in face of Tibullus' poetic achievement.

Thus far we have been talking about the contents of Tibullus' poems, about his skill in communicating his emotional states, and about his graphic skill in general. A few words concerning his language are now in order. We have referred to the basic sincerity of our poet, who seeks to find his image in the world about him. It does not surprise us that this sincerity is reflected in Tibullus' use of language. His manner of writing is constantly controlled, forever restrained. He writes in what the Alexandrians called the "slender style." For us today this is pretty much tantamount to a simple style. He employs a noticeable purity of diction, which renders his elegies immediately comprehensible and clear to his readers. To be more specific, Tibullus' syntax, for example, is perfectly straightforward. In Propertius we often have to work backward, i.e., we must first try to determine meaning and then twist and adapt his syntax to our predetermined sense. Not so with Tibullus. We rarely puzzle in our levels of expectation as a result of his syntax. Rather his syntactic structures flow as easily and logically as do usually his transitions from theme to theme within any poem. Further, his use of imagery is noteworthy. At the time that Tibullus wrote there had come into being a definite erotic vocabulary employing colloquialisms, often half-vulgar, endearing diminutives, and various stock phrases. Tibullus avoids these; to use them would betray his sincerity.

As for his comparisons, Tibullus is careful that they not get out of hand. Their pertinence is purposefully limited in scope. The similes and metaphors illustrate the material at hand and do not lead the reader to extend them beyond their environment. This is not to say that they are primarily decorative. They do contribute to the emotional impact at their point of occurrence. But having done this, their function is complete. Propertius, on the other hand, sustains and draws out his comparisons—even throughout an entire poem. They often are, in fact, a part of the poem's total structure. Similarly, his frequent mythological allusions are complicated and obscure and again bear upon structure. Tibullus, however, is sparing in his use of such allusions, and when he does employ them, he taps only enough of the myth to serve the immediate purpose.

Actually, this same discreet economy of expression is found in Tibullus' treatment of themes and moods. He always dwells upon a given theme or mood just enough to enable the reader to gain insight and to respond emotionally. But he does not overstate. He does not have to, for his themes and moods are as simple as his use of language. But they *are* of paramount importance for him, and the modern reader must appreciate them with this in mind.

Let us now consider the question of unity. At the end of the sixteenth century the humanist Joseph Scaliger thought that Tibullus' verses, having passed through the hands of careless copyists, were spread about like pieces of broken glass. He and scholars after him tried to put "order" and "meaning" into the elegies by arranging the verses in different ways. Some modern critics, however, would not even go this far. They categorically affirm that the poetry of Tibullus is devoid of unity. What both early and modern critics have failed to realize is that the various thematic elements of Tibullus' poetry do create a whole which is full of a very special inner harmony. The unity is clearly not thematic, but rather emotional, similar to the unity of a musical composition. Any given theme or mood may momentarily emerge and predominate, only to give way to other themes and moods. And when one reads the two books of Tibullus as a whole, one can see that these themes are actually leitmotifs, constantly being echoed and re-echoed. All are part of the poet's very existence, and it is indicative of his poetic skill that the modern reader can identify with the lonely situation of a man who wanted so little and yet so much out of life—to be loved.

We have seen that Tibullus was a member of Messalla's literary circle. The manuscripts which have transmitted to us Tibullus' two books of elegies also contain the works of other members of this circle, and a few words should be said about these poems. They have been grouped into two books since the sixteenth century, although originally they made up only one. Together with Tibullus' own two books these other two constitute the collection which we call the *Corpus Tibullianum*. The six poems of Book III were written by one Lygdamus. The name is probably a pseudonym, and many attempts have been made to identify the poet with various contemporary literary figures. He writes of a certain well-born Neaera, whose love he tries to regain. The poet shows few signs of true inspiration and his technical skill leaves much to be desired. In general he impresses us as being an amateur poet. Book IV opens with a long eulogy of Messalla written in dactylic hexameters. It is a rather tasteless, ostentatious attempt of some unknown sycophant to gain Messalla's favor. The following five poems, known collectively as the "Garland of Sulpicia," treat of the lady's love for one Cerinthus. Sulpicia herself wrote the next half dozen short elegies in which she expresses her love for the man. Although the poetess also shows traces of amateurishness, her poems are of more significant literary value than those of Lygdamus. She is successful in communicating her emotions to the reader. We detect a tender warmth in her frank expression of passionate love for Cerinthus.

It has been thought that Tibullus himself wrote not only the "Garland of Sulpicia" but also the last two poems in the fourth book. Horace mentions Tibullus' love affair with one Glycera (*Odes* I,33), and conceivably the last two poems in the *Corpus Tibullianum* refer to this love. But since Glycera is not mentioned by name, the establishment of Tibullan authorship remains a matter of conjecture.

All of the poems in the last two books are bound to suffer when compared with the authentic Tibullan output. Still, we are fortunate that they have come down to us, for they give us an insight into the variety of composition current within Messalla's literary circle. Tibullus, of course, is the luminary of that circle, and from ancient times his literary talent was noted and appreciated. Upon the death of Tibullus, Domitius Marsus asserted that the love elegy had lost its great master. The statement is all the more impressive considering the fact that Propertius was still living. Also occasioned by Tibullus' death were the verses of his fellow elegist, Ovid:

> Aurora lamenting for Memnon, Thetis in tears for Achilles—
> Even a goddess can mourn sorrowful fates of mankind.
> Elegy, loosen your hair: weep for the lot of Tibullus. . . .
> *Amores* III.9.1ff., trans. Rolfe Humphries

Ovid gives us another tribute to Tibullus elsewhere in the *Amores* (I, 15, 276.). Here he refers to Tibullus as "elegant" (*cultus*) and predicts in effect that as long as there are love and lovers, people will cultivate his poetry. By calling Tibullus "elegant," Ovid tries to describe the various features of the poet's style which we have already noticed. Quintilian attempts the same in the remainder of the passage to which we earlier referred:

> In the genre of Elegy also we compete with the Greeks. Of our poets of this genre, Tibullus seems to me to be an especially polished and elegant author. There are those who prefer Propertius.
>
> *Inst.* Orat. 10.1.93

Judging from these notices, Tibullus' fame was firmly established in antiquity. As Quintilian points out, there were those who would award the palm to Propertius, and he certainly comes off the better today, for he is more of a poet in our modern sense of the word. But we must be careful not to judge poets—especially ancient poets—comparatively, unless we have grounds for comparison. The experience of each is unique and the poetic *modus operandi* will necessarily vary. Let us try to appreciate Tibullus as Tibullus. As a matter of personal taste we might prefer others over him, but given his personal experience, how successful is our poet in communicating it, and to what extent can we identify with it—these are the questions we must ask in evaluating Tibullus' poetry.

Although apparently popular and well read for many years after his death, Tibullus did eventually fall into oblivion as a result of Ovid's popularity. But with the Renaissance, Tibullus, along with Catullus and Propertius, was rediscovered. The numerous editions throughout the sixteenth and seventeenth centuries attest to his renewed popularity. It would be idle to catalogue the many references and tributes which modern writers have made to Tibullus. Certainly his influence is not of a direct and immediate sort when it comes to the modern development of elegy and lyric poetry in general. But, then, literary influence is frequently of an accumulative nature. In the nineteenth century German elegy made its rise under Goethe. Although Propertius seems to have wielded more tangible influence on him, we may surmise that Tibullus too had his effect. The same applies to Shelley and Tennyson in England, Delille and Parny in France (Voltaire addressed the latter as "Mon cher Tibulle"), and Jimenez in Spain, to mention only a few. It is interesting that in a poem to his friend Batiushkov, Pushkin could state that he was baptized by Tibullus in the name of Apollo. Even in art our poet seems to have left his mark, for Watteau's "Embarcation for Cythera," it is thought, was inspired by Tibullus' depiction of the Elysian Fields in Book I, iii.

The adjective "anaemic," used to describe Tibullus and his poetry, is not only misleading, but also unfair. This erroneous judgment stems from a misunderstanding of our poet's skilled, intentional restraint in writing—his "slender style." Also contributory has been the misunderstanding of Tibullus' manipulation of his themes. But if we permit Tibullus to say what he has to say in the way he chooses to say it, if we arrive at a plausible understanding of his emotional problems, then for all of his superficial simplicity and rambling, we shall detect in his poetry not anaemia, but rather a unique vitality. And it is the unique merit of Constance Carrier's translation that his vitality can be felt in English verse. The translator employs, as in her Propertius translations, alternating rhymes. Her frames are again exact and her transitions from one to the other are facile. No less noteworthy is the limpid flow of her English verse—her sensitivity to rhythm. As a result of her translation the modern reader will conclude that Tibullus was a "body with very much soul." And he will be able to appreciate what Mörike had in mind when he wrote:

> Just as the shifting wind will whisk through the
> tender seedlings
> bent into swaying dance toward all directions at once,
> O love-stricken Tibullus! So rhapsodically, so with
> magic your songs stream forth, while you're
> besieged by the God.

trans. E. George (unpubl.)

EDWARD M. MICHAEL

Haverford College
April, 1967

NOTES

1. The vocabulary in the anonymous *Life* is clearly post-classical. The compiler may have used the life of Tibullus in the *De Poetis,* a section of Suetonius' *De Viris Illustribus,* no longer extant.
2. Tibullus is referred to as *iuvenis* in the epigram and *adolescens* in the *Vita.*
3. *Odes* I,33.
4. *Tristia* IV,10,51-54.
5. *Epistles* I,4,2.
6. Apuleius states (*Apol.* 10) that Delia's real name was Plania. It has been suggested that she was of plebeian origin.
7. Since it was a literary convention of the elegists to consider themselves poor, we must not take Tibullus' references to his poverty too seriously. Although his material resources were reduced as a result of the confiscations of 42 B.C., we may assume that he continued to live a comfortable life.

NOTE ON THE TEXT

The Latin text used for this translation is the Loeb Classical Library edition.

BOOK ONE

I, i

DIVITIAS ALIUS FULVO SIBI CONGERAT AURO...

Others may cherish their hoard, gold the color of sunlight,
keep for themselves alone plowed and productive acres,
live in trembling fear of enemies at their portal,
hearing in every sound warnings to break their slumber,
if I may move in peace, poor in all but contentment,
warmed by a little blaze flickering on the hearthstone.
Here in this narrow range, I shall savor it wholly,
never set forth to make journeys into the darkness;
be sheltered from August's heat in the cool of apple-tree shadow,
hearing the sound of the brook slipping like silk beside me;
never too proud or ashamed to hoe an acre and plant it,
hurry the slow ox with a branch for goad, or carry
home in my arms ewe-lamb or kid found bleating and frightened,
left by its dam, abandoned, lost in the underbrush.
Keeping the seasons' rhythm, I'll plant vines in my garden—
fruit-trees too, like a man born with a true green thumb.

Pray that I may not know harvests other than gracious,
granting me grain for bread, wine for the jars that wait it.
Always I kneel and worship every flowering garland
set on a stump in the fields, decking a crossroads marker;
always the first of the fruit ripening on the branches
goes to the guardian god,[1] offer of thanks for kindness.
Yellow-haired Ceres, bless this farm! I shall hang a garland,
made of the spiky ears of corn, before your altar.
Red Priapus, stand guard over this fruit-rich garden;
swinging your scythe, frighten birds away from the crop.
Gods who protect my house, shielding the little within it,
(once it throve, but no more)—Lares, receive your honors.
Years when our flocks were large, you would be given a heifer:
all that the farm affords now is a humble lamb.
For you a lamb shall die; around the altar you'll hear them,
farmboys shouting *Hurrah! Send us a fine harvest!*
You, in return, O spare my flock from wolves and from robbers;
let them steal from herds larger and better than mine
which must provide for my shepherd all of the rites of cleansing
and as well for all the milk-offerings made to Pales.
Gods, be with me; accept gifts from my humble table
poured into earthen cups, set on a scoured board.
Such were the cups the first countryman made to drink from,
shaping them with his hands out of the pliant clay.
I am not hungering for wealth like my grandfather's—
crops and the sale of crops, money that makes money.
All that I want is a small field and what it produces;
enough so long as I sleep sound on my hard mattress.
Who would not envy me, holding my love in my arms,
warm in the winter night, hearing the wild winds rage—
or, when the cold South wind blows and the rain hisses,
both of us sound asleep, lulled by the storm's wailing.
This is the fate I choose. He who would have a fortune—
he must pay its toll, learn to face gale and shipwreck.

I would rather that all the gems in the world should vanish
than that I leave a girl mourning a fortune-seeker.
You, Messalla—your way is to deck your house with the trophies
brought to it from wars fought in distant countries.
I cannot wander, chained prisoner of her beauty,
doorkeeper set before doors that are barred to me.
Delia, my dear delight, you are the glory I yearn for.
"Wastrel"—I welcome the slur, spending my life in love.
Yours is the face I would see, my last hour upon me;
yours is the hand I would hold, talisman and touchstone;
yours the tears that would almost quench the flames at my bier.
Tears and kisses together, mingled bitter and tender!
Weep—I know that you will; who's more tender than Delia?
May no man nor maid turn from that burial dry-eyed.
Spare my spirit grief; yet be sparing with outward
signs of sorrow, my darling—needless to loose your hair,
needless to let your tears mark those delicate cheeks.
Meanwhile O come close! Love, make us one in living;
dark-hooded Death will come all too soon to part us,
all too soon we'll grow old; Love will find us grotesque, then,
palsied and white-headed, mouthing the speech of Love.
Now is our day, our night—shameless, I'll break down doors,
out of sheer joy in life stir up a lively brawl.
In this war I am both officer and recruit;
down with bugles and flags! Wounds and wealth to the greedy!
Safe with all I could want, why should I envy such?
Hunger and hunger for money—I can despise them both.

I, ii
ADDE MERUM VINOQUE NOVOS COMPESCE DOLORES...

More wine, more wine, to wash away new troubles,
to let sleep triumph and my eyelids close;
and when I lie there, my flushed temples throbbing,
do not break in on that ill-starred repose.
She might as well be jailed, so well they watch her—
spied on and locked away, and mine no more!
Rain, lash the door of that stone-hearted guardian!
Jove, aim your thunder at that bolted door!
Door, hear my plaint and open to me only;
in stealth, in silence, let me enter in.
If I have spoken ill of you, or cursed you,
let it be on my own head now, that sin.
Think of the phrases I've rehearsed before you,
the flowers I've brought to make your threshold gay.
Keep up your courage, Delia; trick your jailer—
Love laughs at locksmiths, so the wise men say:
Venus will help a shy lad as he fumbles
the lock, a girl who lifts a muffled latch;
will show how best to slip from bed unnoticed
with steps whose sound no listening ear can catch;
to give a lover, while the husband listens,
with each chaste word a promise or a sign.
Venus does all of this, but for those only
the limit of whose love no fears define.
See how I wander all night through the city
and never come to harm—she is my shield;
by her grace none may steal my cloak or wallet;
against attack her strength will keep me steeled.
Her bondsmen move unscathed through every danger,

no ambush ever takes them unaware.
I walk through winter nights and scarcely shiver,
the cold rain soaks me and I do not care.
And what would cure me now? My Delia's finger
at the opened gate, to summon me inside.
Look elsewhere when we pass you, men and women
in the night streets; Love's thefts are his to hide.
Do not come running after us with torches,
asking our names, prying and Argus-eyed.[2]
Or if, unseen, you see us, never say so;
let such encounters vanish from your mind.
Venus is born of blood and of the ocean,[3]
as any loose-mouthed chatterer will find.
Such gossip Delia's husband will not credit—
the kindly witch I pray to gives her oath:
fixed stars and rushing streams are in her power,
a power that can change the course of both.
Her chant can reach the dead and wake the spirits
and from the pyre call bones charred by its heat;
keening, she keeps the ghostly troop before her,
or, sprinkling them with milk, bids them retreat.
If it's her whim, she'll chase the clouds from heaven
or into ice the air of June congeal;
she knows the herbs that made Medea's witchcraft;
she brings the hounds of Hecate to heel.
This charm she taught me, so that you might trick him—
sing the words three times through, then three times spit.
So, if he hears we go to bed together—
or even sees—he'll put no faith in it.
Be careful, though; it's I must be the lover
if he's the cuckold, else he won't be blind.
Why do I trust her? It was she who promised
to free my love by spells she had designed;

she cleansed me with a ritual of torches
and made by night her sorcerer's sacrifice.
I prayed, not to be free of, but to share love;
if I'm your slave, then slavery's worth the price.
A man who had your love would be inhuman
if he would leave to lead a regiment
or chase Cilicia's routed troops before him
or pitch on conquered land his martial tent,
posturing as a hero, mounted, armored,
he and his horse all glittering in gold.
His choice be such, but mine to live with Delia,
yoke oxen, lead my flocks from hill to fold,
to hold her close, my still-young arms around her,
our slumber soft upon a bed of stone.
What good are silken sheets and goose-down pillows
if a man lies there wakeful and alone?
Without her, even the drowsy sound of waters,
the softest bed, could never give me sleep.
O Venus, have my speeches wronged your godhead?
is it my words' rash harvest that I reap?
am I accused of entering the temple,
of stealing garlands from that holy shrine?
I'll fling myself full-length upon its threshold
and kiss it humbly, if that fault is mine;
I'll crawl upon the floor to do my penance
and beat my head against the sacred door.
Take care, you who would ridicule my sorrows:
the gods in time may even up the score.
I've seen a man who mocked unlucky young love
put his own senile neck in Cupid's noose,
murmur endearments in a fatuous quaver,
and dye his hair—with love as his excuse;
unblushing, doting, hang around her doorstep
or bribe her maid, accosted in the square,

while boys and young men crowd and thrust and jostle,
baring their own soft breasts and spitting there.[4]

Be gentle, Venus. Hear the songs I sing,
nor, angered, burn the offerings I bring.

I, iii

IBITIS AEGEAS SINE ME, MESSALLA, PER UNDAS...

Messalla, will you go without me through the Aegean?
Do not forget me there, my guard, my other self!
Phaeacia holds me back, sick in a foreign country—
Death with your greedy hands, Death, black Death, hold off!
Hold off, black Death, I beg; my mother is far away;
she cannot gather my burned bones to her grieving breast.
I have no sister here to sprinkle my ashes with perfume,
nor to weep by my grave, her hair dishevelled and tossed.
Neither is Delia near, who would not let me leave her
till she was reassured by the gods of my return.
Three times she lifted the lots from the boy's hands, and three times
reading the lots, he said she would have no reason to mourn.[5]
No hint of danger at all, and yet irrational terror,
in the days before the journey, left her in tears and afraid,
till I was troubled too, though I tried to give her comfort—
and did my best to find reasons to stay, instead.
Those birds were an evil omen, that word was unlucky, I murmured,
or, *It's only asking for trouble to start on Saturn's day.*[6]
Sometimes I got as far as the gate before I stumbled,
and then, *Bad luck!* I cried, and there was relief in the cry.
No man in his senses will leave as long as love is unwilling;
let him set out, he'll find the god is blocking his path.
O Isis whom Delia worships,[7] what help can you bring her lover?
the cymbals that her hands clashed—will they hold off my death?
what good are the nights that Delia gave to the rites of the goddess,
bathing in clear water, to sleep in a separate bed?
Help me, Isis! I've seen, drawn on the walls of your temple,
pictures of votaries who have been given your aid.
Help me, that Delia may pay the nightly vigils she vowed you,
sitting in linen robes in front of your holy door,

coming twice a day for your Egyptians to gape at,
chanting her praise of the goddess, humbly, with unbound hair.
Help me, that I may come to stand at my family altars
offering, every month, payment of incense to Lar.
People were better off in the days of Saturn's kingship[8]
before the world was opened out to the traveler!
The pine-tree had not yet learned to scorn the blue sea-waters
nor to hold up the sail that billows out in the wind;
no sailor, hoping for loot, had ventured to unknown countries
or loaded the hold of his ship with the foreign wares he found.
The bull had not known the yoke, his fierceness was still unbroken;
not yet had human hand set harness upon the horse;
no one had thought of doors; no man used boundary markers
to set his neighbor's acres apart from those that were his.
Honey dropped from the oak; ewes with heavy udders
came uncalled to the shepherd at the close of day.
Those times knew no wars, no blood-lust rousing to battle;
there was no smith to forge weapons that men should die.
But our god is Jupiter, now, a god of warfare and carnage;
the sea can slay, and death has a thousand ways to come.
Spare me, Jove! I need not tremble at promises broken;
I have no cause to fear as they do who blaspheme,
but if my days are done, the span that the gods allot me,
set over my bones a stone, engraved in a clear hand:
HERE TIBULLUS LIES, WHOM DEATH SEIZED AS HE FOLLOWED,
OVER THE LAND AND OVER THE SEA, MESSALLA, HIS FRIEND.
It will be Venus herself (she has always found me faithful)
who will lead me along the way to the Elysian fields
where song and dancing go on forever, and overhead, curving
and fluting and falling, song from the delicate throats of birds.
The fields, untilled, will bear trees of a cinnamon sweetness,
and roses cover the earth and fill the air with their scent.
Young men and girls will meet in sport and easy laughter;
there will be no wars but Love's, waged always on every front.

And here are those whom death robbed of both life and lover,
their mark a wreath of myrtle laid lightly on the hair.
But the Kingdom of the Damned lies deep in a gulf of darkness,
pitchblack, and all around it the pitchblack rivers roar.
Tisiphone is there, with writhing snakes for a headdress;
all the reckless and evil go rushing in aimless flight,
and other wide-mouthed snakes hiss on the head of the watchdog[9]
keeping his sleepless guard before the bronze-bound gate.
Ixion is there, who tried to force his will on Juno;
his guilty body is stretched taut on the turning wheel.
And there is Tityos, spread-eagled over nine acres;
birds tear at his vitals, unsleeping, insatiable.
Tantalus too is here, waist-deep in the pool that always,
when he would gulp its coolness, shrinks from his cracked mouth;
and the Danaids, who fill the leaking jars with water—
flouters of Venus, now they must endure her wrath.
There I consign all those who have held my love in dishonor
and those who wish me away in never-ending war.
Delia, I beg of you, stay true to me in my absence;
give gossip no chance to start; keep your maidservant near;
hear the stories she tells in the quiet lamp-lit evenings
while she holds the distaff, spinning the long thread,
and all around her the others bend to the tasks you have set them,
till sleep comes touching gently mistress as well as maid—
O then let me be at the door, sudden and unreported,
so that it seems to you I have dropped from the sky,
and O come running out to meet me, breathless and barefoot,
your bright hair blown like a flag—O Delia, welcome me!
This is my only prayer: star in the brightening blue,
Dawn, driving your rosy horses,[10] O make it true!

I, iv

SIC UMBROSA TIBI CONTINGANT TECTA, PRIAPE...

May a leafy covert shelter you, Priapus,
and neither storm nor hot sun bring you harm.
Shockheaded and thickbearded, you have captured
our handsome lads—by trick? by magic charm?
Naked you bear the icy winds of winter,
naked the Dogstar's days of parching sun.
The farm god born of Bacchus gave me answer,
armed with his curved billhook, when I had done.
"Trust to no gentle band of boys," he told me.
"They give you too much reason to grow fond—
one by his skill at reading will attract you;
one, swimming strongly in a quiet pond;
one by his young and touching self-assurance,
and one, perhaps, still shy enough to blush.
If he refuse at first, do not be troubled;
this capture's something that you must not rush—
it's time that teaches men to master lions,
it's time that helps the stream wear down the stone.
The turning year brings grapes to sunny hillsides;
the zodiac keeps a pattern of its own.
Swear any oath—love's perjuries are empty,
so light that winds can bear them through the air.
Thank Jove for that; by his decree no lover
need keep the pledge that love has made him swear,[11]
though he has sworn upon Dictynna's arrows,
no matter, or upon Minerva's hair.[12]
But slowness—that's the danger! Youth goes by us
too swiftly, nor returns, nor stays at rest;
how quickly faded are the earth's bright colors,
how early gone the poplar's leafy crest!

How we forget, once age has slowed those hoofbeats,
the horse that once flashed from the starting-line!
I've watched a young man, feeling time's hand on him,
think of his early follies and repine.
The gods are cruel. A snake, skin shed, emerges
anew, but beauty cannot be reborn.
Apollo and Bacchus—they are young forever,
they only, with their curling hair unshorn.
Whatever it may be your lad asks of you,
do not refuse. Love gains by what love yields.
Go where he goes—a thousand miles or farther,
under the August sun that burns the fields
or under skies grown dark and heavy-clouded,
marked with the colored bow that threatens rain.[13]
If he would skim the blue waves in a light boat,
take up your oar and row with might and main.
Share in the goals he sets, and do not weary—
your hands, grown calloused, will have learned new skills.
If he would hunt throughout the valley, help him
carry the nets, and set them where he wills,
or if he challenge you to fence, accept him,
and—subtly—see that he's the one to win.
His guard once down, take the long-dreamed-of kisses,
himself the victim of the nets you spin.
And if he's coy at first, he'll grow less chary,
until you come to give and he to plead.
But these are decadent days; the gentlest boy now
demands a gift outright, with barefaced greed.
Who can have taught such haggling tricks to lovers?
Mark his unhallowed grave with a black stone!
Learning the lore of poets—this will last you
beyond the golden bribe. Make these your own:
the purple lock of Nisus,[14] Pelops' shoulder
of ivory[15]—verse keep these things alive;

while there are oaks and stars and running water,
the man the Muses tell of still shall thrive.
But he who's deaf to song, who sells his favors,
must wander homeless over Cretan hills,
follow behind the chariot of Cybele
or slash himself while Phrygian music shrills.[16]
Venus approves allurements and caresses,
favors all suppliants, pities every tear."
These things the god would have me sing to Titius[17]
if Titius' wife would only let him hear.
O well, obey her! I'll find other pupils
tricked by some crafty boy, their pride still sore.
No man but has some fame: mine's in advising
the lovelorn patient at my open door.
At eighty I'll still be the old campaigner—
young men may guide my steps, but I'll lead them.
O Marathus, you make my love slow torture;
what use are wiles, what use is stratagem?
Spare me, I beg you; let me not be railed at
as one who tried to teach an art he failed at!

I, v

ASPER ERAM ET BENE DISCIDIUM ME FERRE LOQUEBAR...

Angry, I've sworn and sworn I'd bear this parting—
but boastfulness has gone, and here I stand,
whirled like a top on level ground set spinning
from the coiled string in a boy's practiced hand.
Bring brands and whips for so uncouth a creature;
teach him to hold his tongue, to stop his brag.
Forgive me, by the secret bonds that link us,
by the shared bed, the love that does not flag.
They said it was my prayers that made death free you
when you were almost past the gates of hell;
I purified the air with scattered sulphur
while the old woman sang her magic spell;
I pacified the nightmares come to haunt you—
not once but three times offering meal well-blest;
then, hooded and unbelted, made my nine vows
to Hecate, with all the world at rest.
All I could do I did, and you betray me.
He'll have the girl I ransomed back from death.
All my wild dreams of joy, with you recovered—
at the gods' NO, they vanish in a breath:
"A little house, and Delia watching over
grain on the threshing floor in sunlit dust,
or over grapes piled till the troughs are brimming
and the quick feet tread out the fragrant must.
She'll learn to count the flocks; the servants' baby
she'll teach, and talk to it, and dry its tears;
she'll give the harvest gods, for vines, a cluster,
for flocks, drink-offering, for corn, spiked ears.
Heart of the house, she'll love its things, its people,
while I—being nothing, I shall be at ease.

And when," I said, "my friend Messalla visits,
Delia shall pick him fruit from chosen trees.
Knowing his greatness, she will pay him homage,
cook a fine meal, act as his serving-maid."
Such tales I told myself . . . Blown to the world's end
by any passing wind, the bright dreams fade.
Wine could not bring them back, nor ease my grieving;
wine only sharpened sorrow, and I wept.
The thought of you would drain my lust, and leave me
no good to any girl with whom I slept—
and who, insulted, spread the shameful story
that I'm bewitched and by the devil taught.
Bewitched indeed, by spells not of your speaking
but of your arms, your soft hair loosely caught.
Though you're as lovely as the sea-blue Thetis
riding a bridled dolphin to her prince,[18]
your love is death. The old hag planned my downfall,
and you have been unfaithful ever since.
May her food be bloody, and her lips, stained by it,
find every dish they touch full of its reek;
let her be haunted, too, by ghostly wailing,
and from her roof screech-owl and vulture shriek.
Hunger, drive her to gnaw the weeds in graveyards
or bones from which the wolves have turned aside;
send her to wail, half-naked, through the cities,
a troop of wild dogs snarling at her side.
A god directs it thus—gods guide all lovers;
Venus, enraged, breaks those who break her laws.
O Delia, leave that devil and her teaching.
Of all love's griefs, gold is the first great cause—
a penniless man is faithful, first to seek you,
unflaggingly devoted to your whim;
penniless, he is still your bold protector
clearing your path—what threat are crowds to him?

Penniless, he will serve you, draw your sandals,
their muddied lacings loose, from your white feet.
Why do I sing? The filled hand's knock is answered
at that same door where words must vainly beat.
But you my rival, fear to fall as I did.
Fate's wheel revolves and will not be denied.
Another hopeful's waiting on that doorstep,
and not in vain; stares straight ahead, would hide,
pretends to pass the house, then runs back to it
and coughs (is it a signal?) just outside.
What next? Love's bag of tricks is never-failing.
Snatch every pleasure while there's still smooth sailing.

I, vi

SEMPER UT INDUCAR BLANDOS OFFERS MIHI VULTUS...

Smiling and beckoning, Love, you call me toward you—
and suddenly rail at your poor trustful dupe.
What have I to do with your cruelty? To such follies,
such tricks and snares, would any true god stoop?
The net is spread for me; my faithless Delia
takes a new lover to her bed tonight.
O, she denies it, but she's past believing—
cuckolded, I must share her husband's plight.
I was the fool who taught her how to hoodwink
his guards, and now alas am tricked in turn.
I taught her to evade his arms, and, silent,
to slip away—O she was quick to learn!—
and how with herbs and ointments to mask over
the marks upon her flesh my kisses made.
And you, the husband she deceives so lightly,
who thinks of her as one I might degrade—
better forbid those hours of talk with young men,
that graceful posing with her breast half-bare;
watch for the nods she gives across the table,
the signs her wine-wet finger traces there;
worry when she stays out, or when she tells you
she must serve the goddess where no man may fare.[19]
Trust her to me. I'll lead her to that altar
and risk the power that makes profaners blind.
O I remember how, to touch her finger,
I'd judge her ring and how it was designed;
and how you'd drink my wine, neat, till you nodded,
while I stayed sober, water in my glass.
Forgive the acknowledged wrong. It was not willful.
Love (and who fights love?) made the rules, alas!

To tell the truth, a truth I'm not ashamed of,
I was the one your dog barked at that night.
A lovely wife's no use to one whose treasures,
poor fool, no key can ever lock from sight.
You hold her, but her thoughts are with her lover—
wait: see how suddenly her head will ache!
I'd guard her, though, believe me. Shackles, torture,
flesh torn by whips—I'd bear death for her sake.
Stand back, you worriers about your hair-style,
you fashion-plates, your togas floating wide!
If you should see us, lest you sin by looking,
stand back, or turn aside!

The god himself commands our act; the priestess
instructs us, and the voice is not her own—
as if Bellona drove her, she fears nothing:
flesh-eating flame nor scourge that bares the bone;
she'll gash her arms until her blood has spattered
the fane, and give no sign of suffering;
she will stand there, dagger-pierced, will stand there, bleeding,
and sing the chant she has been taught to sing:
"See that you harm no girl if Love's her guardian,
lest, dogged by misery, you see you've sinned;
touch her, and luck will leave you, like the life-blood
leaving my wound, or ashes blown by wind."
For you too, Delia, she foretold the torment
should you prove false—I pray it may be light,
not for your own sake, no, but for your mother's,
whose goodness almost cures me of my spite.
Trembling, she takes me to you in the darkness;
in frightened silence there she joins our hands;
and when I leave at last, she knows my footstep
as it draws near the doorway where she stands.
Dear lady, live forever. All my own years,

could I bestow them, would be yours to take.
You I love always, and, for you, your daughter.
What could I not forgive her for your sake?
Teach virtue to her, though she does not wear
the robes and fillets that would mark her wed.
Punish me too, if I should praise another—
call down all Delia's fury on my head.
Let her seize me by the hair if she suspect me;
let me be flung forth, though I'm innocent.
And if in madness, love, I ever strike you,
cut off the hand that moves with such intent.
From loyalty, not fear, be chaste, my darling,
and in my absence let love keep you true.
For she who breaks her faith—the years will bow her
and give her shaking hands mean tasks to do—
weave twisted yarn, thread looms, struggle at carding
the clean wool, for some pittance of a wage,
while young girls mock her in a giggling chorus
and say that such a youth reaps such an age.
From the gods' mountain[20] Venus looks on, weeping,
warning the false to learn from such a sight.
Let her curse them. We shall be love's exemplar
even when our hair is white.

I, vii

HUNC CECINERE DIEM PARCAE FATALIA NENTES...

The Fates have sung of this day, the Fates, intent on their spinning—[21]
and none, not even a god, may break that thread.
This is the day on which we routed Aquitania
and crossed the Atax, that trembled at our tread.
The Fates sang true, and today Rome celebrates new triumphs,
while the shackled Gallic chiefs pass, pair by pair.
In an ivory chariot drawn by matched and milk-white horses,
Messalla wears the laurel that victors wear.
Not without me was that glory won where the Pyrenees
beyond the harbor town rise dark and tall.[22]
I have seen the rivers, sluggish or swift, of Spain and Helvetia,
and the slow blue streams that wind through northern Gaul;
I could sing of the Cydnus, too, whose waves, sky-colored, move slowly,
imperceptibly, on toward the calm lagoon,
or of that Asian peak, home of long-haired Cilicians,
Taunus, whose top can blot out stars and moon.
I could tell you as well, if I chose, how that dove the Syrians worship[23]
flies without fear of harm from town to town;
how Tyre, long long ago, with the help of wind and current,
mastered the sea on which its towers look down;[24]
or how, in Egypt's heat, when the Dogstar parches the country,
the Nile runs deep, and men and land are fed.
Father of waters, what is the land I may call your birthplace,
what reason give that you have hidden your head?[25]
There is no need, with your bounty, for Egypt to pray for showers;
no dry brown grass need beg for the gift of rain.
The river-god and Osiris—theirs is a double altar
where hymns to the ox make a wild barbaric strain.[26]

It was Osiris in truth who was the plow's inventor,
turning the virgin earth with an iron share;
he was the first to drop seed in the furrow, and gather
from nameless trees the fruit they began to bear.
He learned, and taught to men, how the vine is tied to the pole,
and how the hook must lop the leaves from the vine.
Out of the grape clusters that heavy feet had trampled,
none before him had ever brought forth wine—
and men, having drunk it, were moved to what would someday be
singing,
once they had smoothed it out, and to rustic dance.
Even today when the farmer finds his burdens too heavy
it is wine that softens his sorry circumstance.
Wine can free man's spirit, can drown out even the clanking
of the iron chains that rub his body raw.
Osiris, yours was never a province of misfortune;
in your land love and mirth and song are law—
ever-blossoming flowers, wreaths of the berried ivy,
yellow robes that swirl with the dancers' feet,
purple robes, and a chest of secret and holy objects,
and a pipe whose music rises thin and sweet.
Come, O come! with a hundred games, with fresh libations,
with dances, invoke the spirit of this place—
let the sweet-smelling ointment drip from his hallowed hair
and his head and neck let weightless garlands grace.
Come to us, Spirit,[27] accept the incense I lay before you,
and the little cakes made sweet with honey from Greece.
But for Messalla, may his chair be ringed by his children;
may his glory and fame with theirs increase;
and let him not be silent on that great work, the roadway
through Tusculum's fields, where the Alban ruins lie.[28]
Your generosity made it, that road of hard-packed gravel
or of flint-blocks joined so close they deceive the eye.
Your is the name the farmer shall praise on his night journeys,

home at last and having met no ill.
But you, Spirit born of this place, return, let us do you honor,
brighter and brighter come, and brighter still!

I, viii

NON EGO CELARE POSSUM, QUID NUTUS AMANTIS...

I know the meaning of a lover's nod,
the whisper meant for a beloved ear—
yet lots, nor entrails showing heaven's will,
nor bird-notes tell me what I have to fear,
Venus it is whose magic binds my arms,
whose whips that scourge me make her precepts clear.

Heaven has fiercer fires for its unwilling
victims. Concealment's all to no avail.
What use now, Pholoe, to comb your curls,
or paint your cheeks, or shape your pointed nail?
to change your dress, your shawl, to tie the thong
tight on your sandal? No, your tricks must fail—

it is not you but she whose charms delight,
her face all shining clean, her silky hair
brushed and loose-hanging. Have you been bewitched
by some hag's spells, breathed on the black night-air?
Evil like that can lead crops from the fields
and halts the hissing snake where it would fare;

can—if the echoing bronze is left unstruck—[29]
try even to draw the moon down from the sky.
Why then should I complain of spell-born woe?
All magic tricks true beauty can put by.
Touch is the root of danger—in the kiss,
in bodies breast to breast and thigh to thigh.

And yet I would not have you turn him down.
For such acts Venus has her punishments.

But beg no gifts—it is an old man's need,
by bribing, to break down indifference;
a young man gives himself, smooth face, clear skin—
and who could ask for more munificence?

Around those polished shoulders put your arms
and you will own the treasures of a king.
Venus will find a way for secret love,
set him to touch your breasts, and, quivering,
to kiss with lips and tongue, insatiable,
and bruise the throat with prints that teethmarks bring.

What good are jewels or gold to any girl
no man desires, who must sleep alone?
But it is age that really values love—
seeks to call back again what it has known,
stares in the mirror, tints the hair with dyes,
tests every nostrum made from nut or bone—

tries to pull out the white hairs by the root
each morning, in a kind of endless race;
or puts himself into the surgeon's hands
and comes forth with a strange and unlined face.
There is our future, closing, closing in;
while it is still spring, let us claim its grace.

Marathus loves you. Why be cruel to him?
who deserves cruelty except the old?
If he looks jaundiced, love has made him ill—
no cause to shun him, or reproach, or scold.
Hear how he weeps for her who will not hear—
he'll flood us out unless he is consoled!

"Why does she scorn me? We could trick the guard.

Love teaches lovers how to be unheard,
and I have learned to steal a kiss, to breathe,
so gently you would swear that nothing stirred—
to come at midnight and unbar the door
and never frighten even the shyest bird.

But what are all these talents if the girl
refuse her lover and forsake his bed?
or, if she promises and breaks her word,
what can I do but weep all night instead,
straining my ears and hoping every creak
is not a simple creak but her light tread?"

No good to mourn, my boy. Her heart is stone.
If you weep so, why, you compound your pain.
I warn you, Pholoe, no sacrifice
will be enough atonement for disdain.
And you, lad, whom the great god overheard
mocking unlucky love, repent in vain.

Do you recall those jests, or how you teased
your lover with excuses and delay?
Now you hate coyness; now you beat the door
that with its bolts and latches bars your way.
And you, girl, mend your ways or wait your penance—
the time may come when you'll wish back this day.

I, ix

QUID MIHI, SI FUERAS MISEROS LAESUROS AMORES...

If you meant to deny my passion,
why make that pledge at the altar
and break it secretly?
For a while the perjury's hidden,
but punishment stalks your steps.
Be merciful, gods; his beauty
can be forgiven one sin.
For money, farmers harness
the ox to plow their land;
gain-seeking ships are guided
by stars through wind-lashed seas.
Bribes have seduced Marathus—
may they turn to water and ash!
He will beg forgiveness, all dust-stained,
his hair made rough by the wind,
burned by the sun, and limping
on travel-blistered feet.
I warned him, "Keep beauty sacred;
gold is a mine of grief.
When love is betrayed for money,
Venus is suddenly cold.
Rather burn my head, or stab me,
or scourge my bleeding back.
If you plan harm, do not conceal it—
the gods will make it plain.
A trusted slave can babble,
drunk, if they so decree;
and sleeping lips may murmur
what, waking, they would hide."
I argued and wept and—shameful!—

flung myself at your feet,
and you swore that neither for money
nor jewels would you break your word,
not even for all Campania
or Falernum and its wine.
I would have denied, at your bidding,
that rivers run downhill.
When you wept, I believed your weeping,
and, credulous, dried your tears.
It's Pholoe now you cherish—
may she learn deceit from you!
That none might know of your wooing
how often I lighted your way
or brought her to you and waited,
face hidden, outside the door.
What a fool I was to pander!
I should have guessed love's tricks.
The poems I wrote in your honor—
both I and the Muses blush.
Let the Fire-god[30] shrivel my verses
or water wash out the words—
go, leave me. Sell your beauty;
return and brag of the gain.
And you, my lad's corrupter,
may your own wife cuckold you;
worn from adultery, draw up
the sheet, lie lax at your side.
May your bed bear marks of a stranger,
your house be that of a whore;
let her drain both wine and lover
in her insatiate thirst;
let her parties last till daybreak,
or let gossip say they do;
let her be a pattern for harlots,

a preceptor skilled of sex.
But you do not notice her learning,
her new seductive ways—
not for you she arranges
her hair with a golden comb;
your beauty doesn't inspire
her jewels, her purple gown.
Your approval means nothing;
she would damn your house for him.
Yet she's not depraved; her partners
are young; they are free from gout—
more than I'll say for Marathus:
I swear he'd mate with a beast.
You have sold to any bidder
kisses I thought were mine;
you will suffer all my torments
when a new lad takes your place.
In my joy at your grief, I'll offer
Venus a golden palm:
TIBULLUS, FREED FROM HIS BONDAGE,
PRAYS YOU WILL NOTE HIS THANKS.

I, x

QUIS FUIT, HORRENDOS PRIMOS QUI PROTULIT ENSES?...

What man, what devil, first conceived the sword?
shaper of iron, himself an iron heart,
begetter of battles on a innocent world,
marking new routes to death on mankind's chart!
Or did he arm himself for self-defense?
have we demeaned what he used against the beast?
Gold taught us to kill our fellows. There were no wars
when wooden cups stood at the simple feast,
when citadels and palisades were unknown,
and the shepherd slept unfearful among his flocks.
If I could choose an age, I would live in that one,
with no trumpet-call, no war's alarms and shocks.
But I cannot escape; I know that somewhere a foeman
carries the weapon destined for my side.
Save me, gods of my fathers! In my childhood
I played at your altar and knew you as my guide.
Let none despise you, carved from the gnarled wood—
statues my grandfather worshipped years ago,
in days when the humble shrine held rough-hewn figures
in tattered robes, but reverenced even so,
when gods were pleased with the grapes laid on their altars,
or the spiky wreath set on a carven head.
Granted their favor, a man brought cakes of honey;
his child brought honey, walking with careful tread.
Gods, turn away from me those sharp bronze weapons!
I'll offer a fat hog from the farmyard sties.
With a myrtle-decked basket and a wreath of myrtle,
fresh-robed, will I find approval in your eyes?
Let other men, Mars-aided, glory in warfare
and later boast of their feats in the battle line,

while we drink together, and they draw on the table
plans of the camp, with a finger dipped in wine.
Are we mad, to give dark death such invitation?
He is close enough in peace; he comes by stealth;
in his kingdom are only Cerberus and Charon,
no vineyards, no fields, to bring a harvest's wealth;
his people are pale as they wander by dark waters;
their sockets are eyeless; fire has singed their hair.
Give me for hero the man who raises children,
a houseful of them, and sleeps out his old age there—
one son tending the flock, helping his father,
while the wife heats water that they may wash their limbs.
Let me live, like him, till every hair is silvered,
and I tell of a golden past that never dims.
Let Peace watch over our fields—Peace, fair and lucent,
who trained the ox with a curved yoke, bidding it plow,
made vineyards and stored their juice, so that the father
may have pressed the very wine that the son drinks now.
Peace lifts to the sun the hoe and the plowshare; darkness
covers the soldier's broken weapons with rust.
Merry with drink, the farmer drives the cart homeward
with his wife and childen through the sunny dust.
And they make love—not gently; doors are broken
and hair is pulled and the women scream like shrews
and the young girl's cheek is bruised—but the man who struck her
weeps in shame at the sight of the swelling bruise,
and the quarrel fades and kindles, with love to feed it—
love, sitting unconcerned between the pair.
A man is iron, surely, to beat his sweetheart;
he drags the gods to the ground through protesting air.
Forgive him, though, if he tears away her clothing
or tumbles her curls—a girl will cry at this,
but he can make peace. Indeed, how lucky the lover
whose anger rouses tears he can stop with a kiss!

But the cruel-handed have shield and stake to carry;
Venus would flee from the sound of that heavy boot.
Peace, O come to us, holding corn with its tassels,
and pour from the breast of your robe a harvest of fruit!

BOOK TWO

II, i

QUISQUIS ADEST, FAVEAT: FRUGES LUSTRAMUS ET AGROS...

It is our duty, in silence, to purify crops and ground
by the ritual our fathers bequeathed us with the land.
Bacchus, bless with your presence! from your horns hang the clustered grape.
Ceres, wreathe your temples with corn-ears newly ripe.
This is a holy day. Let the plowman take his rest,
work be stopped, and the plowshare gather one day's dust.
Loosen the yoke-straps now; see to it that you put
grain in the manger where the garlanded oxen wait,
for each act today must be an oblation made
to the god—even distaff and wool must be put aside.
There is never a part in these rites for those to have
who come here this morning worn from a night of love.
We must worship undefiled, must wear robes fresh and clean
when we come to the holy spring, and dip our clean hands in.
Straight to the hallowed altar moves the holy lamb;

their hair bound round with olive, the white-clad marchers come.
We would purify, O gods, farmer and fruitful soil,
and beg you to drive from our boundaries all that would bring
us ill,
see that no poor crop shall make our effort vain,
that there be no swift wolf our lambs cannot outrun.
Then, trusting in your goodness and in the abundant earth,
well-content, the farmer can sit before his hearth
where a troop of slave-youngsters, home-born proof of his power,
build their stick-castles before the leaping fire.
Such is my prayer. And now look for the liver-marks
the entrails show to prove that the gods favor our works.[31]
Bring me Falernum's smoky wine from the bin[32]—be sure
the vintage is good—and break the bands on the Chian jar.[33]
Now, with the gods benign, we'll take our holiday:
no need to blush if we're drunk, if our footsteps go awry—
and there's a toast to Messalla each one of us must make,
and we must mention the absent every time we speak.
Messalla, triumphant in Gaul, victor personified,
whose leadership would make your bearded forefathers proud,
be with me, give me your blessing, inspire the words of my song
in praise of those heavenly beings and the earthly treasure they
bring.
This is a hymn for them alone, the country gods
who, when man's only food was acorns, were first his guides:
who taught him to cut trees and shear the branches off
and put the logs together for a house with leaves for a roof;
who, so tradition says, were the first to tame the bull
that man might have a slave; who taught the shape of the wheel
and made the cart—till man put off his primitive ways,
watered his garden, planted his orchard in orderly rows,
gathered the golden juice that trampled grapes would spill,
mixed it with sober water, and drank it to cheer his soul.
The land brings us her fullness, under the sun's fire,

and every autumn leaves her shorn of her yellow hair.
Through the country air in spring bees buzz and hum
and heap the hive with flowers to fill the honeycomb;
the sweaty farmer, tired of plowing in hot noon sun,
would rest in the shade and make words that fitted a tune,
or, his belly full, would finger the stop on an oaten pipe
to win the ear of a god whose image he tried to shape.
It was such a man, great Bacchus, his face vermilion-dyed,
who beat a rustic measure for rustic feet to tread,
and, for a better yield, made an offering worthy of boast:
a he-goat, the flock's leader, the biggest and the best.
Some young farm-boy's rough hands have learned to twine
field-flowers in a circlet, that the god might have a crown.
And still in country pastures today the white sheep browse—
gentle girls will be busy soon with that clipped fleece;
quick, in the way of women, to weigh and card and comb,
using distaff and spindle spun between finger and thumb—
Minerva's faithful servants, with their immemorial song
that blends with the song of the loom, as the clay weights swing.
Where bull and cow graze, and the never-bridled mare—
born, like them, of the fields, is the god who breeds desire;
there in those quiet pastures he aimed his untrained bow
with hands that have grown in skill until they are expert now.
His target has changed as well; now it is men he would tame,
not beasts; he will pierce the hearts of girls well-guarded at home.
He can waste a young man's wealth; he likes to force the old
to stutter in shame, bedevilled by those who will not yield.
He guides the steps of the girl who creeps past her sleeping guard
and slips away to her lover, moving shadow-hidden, unheard,
her nerves tight with fear, testing the path with her foot,
reaching with blind hands through the blackness of the night.
If those who deny the god must bear his punishments.
those on whom Love smiles will never know mischance.
Come, bless our country feast, most holy—but leave behind

your arrows; as for your torch, do not let it fire this land!
Hark when we sing you songs to pray for our flocks' increase
and beg your blessing, aloud, for them; in a whisper, for us—
or aloud for ourselves as well; no man will be able to hear
in that noisy crowd where the curved pipes play a Phrygian air.
Dance, O dance! Night yokes her team,[34] and the golden troop
of stars capers behind their mother, and finally Sleep
comes silently, his dark wings furled, and after him
his Visions, whose images waver like weeds in a running stream.

II, ii

DICAMUS BONA VERBA: VENIT NATALIS AD ARAS...

Speak no evil today, for we honor Cornutus' birth.
Standing here at the altar, be silent, friends!
Burn holy incense now, and from lands at the ends of the earth,
burn for their fragrance the spices Arabia sends.
His guardian-spirit comes to receive of us, if he will,
the crown of flowers gathered from bush and vine,
and the nard to bathe his temples—approving, taking his fill
of honey-cakes, and drunk on unwatered wine.
Then seize your chance, Cornutus! Now whatever you seek
the spirit must grant. Quick, tell your hope! He nods.
It will not be hard to guess your wish before you speak:
your wife's true love. That wish is known to the gods.
No treasure in all the world has a value like this girl's—
not all the wealth the plowman wrests from the fields.
You would not give her up though you were promised the pearls
that the great red sea of blessed India yields.[35]
And your prayers are answered. See! Love with a rustle of wings
lights at your side with bonds that will keep her there—
golden bonds to endure till slow-paced old age brings
lines to her forehead and cheek, and whitens her hair.

Spirit that saw his birth, make his happiness complete:
bless him with many children to tumble and romp at his feet.

II, iii
RURA MEAM, CORNUTE, TENENT VILLAEQUE PUELLAM...

The girl I love, Cornutus, prefers a country home;
is my heart then so hard, that I should stay here in Rome?
Along those green-leafed lanes Venus and Cupid walk
and learn from country people a country turn of talk.
If she were watching me, O with how skilled a hand
would I use the sturdy hoe to work the fertile land,
or follow the curved plow, like a true son of the breed,
while the barren oxen broke the clods to receive the seed!
I would never complain of the white-hot noonday heat
or ask her sympathy for blistered hands and feet.
You tended Admetus' herds once, Apollo beyond compare,[36]
and little use to you then the lyre, the lustrous hair;
no herbs in the world could heal your grief, the grief of one
who has dared Jove's fury for love of a murdered son.
But Phoebus, growing used to his rounds—or so it would seem—
mixed with milk the rennet that would curdle the thick cream;
taught men to bend rushes into a basket-shape
to hold the cheese, leaving space for the whey to escape.
Diana would blush as she met him moving through fields and farms
like any mortal farmer, a stray lamb in his arms;
and when his music sounded from valleys he walked along,
the bellow of the oxen would break on his song.
Troubled chiefs would beg him to make the future plain,
but the crowds would leave his temple, all their prayers in vain.
Often Latona grieved at that roughened sacred hair
which had seemed to his stepmother herself so wondrous fair—[37]
indeed, a man seeing that unwreathed, unkempt head
might have asked, *But where is Apollo? where has the god fled,*
and where is Apollo's Delos, and Delphi's serpent-shrine?
Love lodges the god in a cottage no larger than yours or mine.

Those were happier days when men told how, unashamed,
the gods themselves were pierced by the arrows Love aimed.
We gossip still of his victims—I would rather be gossiped of
as a mortal who loves his girl than a god without a love.
And you, the unknown whom an angry Cupid, to trouble me more,
sends to invade my house and carry on his war

. . . .

We praise not love but loot, in these degenerate days,
yet loot can bring us evil in all of a thousand ways—
buckling madmen's armor, sharpening swords to kill,
hungry for bloodshed, calling death nearer and nearer still.
Loot, or the hope of loot, doubled the sea's threat
when on the rocking boats those warlike prows were set.
Why should a man take over, unless he is spurred by greed,
acre on measureless acre where countless cattle feed?
Why should he carry off great marble columns, torn
from the stripped town and away on creaking wagons borne?
His jetties bound the harbor, so that, to profit him,
heedless of ocean storms great shoals of fish may swim.
The simplest dish is ample to serve my cheerful meal—
pottery from Samos or clay from Cumae's wheel
are enough for me—but nowadays a girl wants golden plates.
So I must seek for loot, while Love impatiently waits;
that through admiring crowds my Nemesis may drift,
beautiful in the jewels and silks that will be my gift.
From Cos she shall have thin gauze, woven in golden bands,
and little dark-skinned page-boys from India's sun-scorched lands,
and the rarest dyes for her dresses, from Africa and Tyre—
scarlet, crimson, purple, all shimmering like fire.
I say nothing new. A man whom crowds now kneel to greet
may once have danced as a slave on gypsum-whitened feet.[38]
You fields which lure away Nemesis from my side,
I'll put a curse upon you till every stalk has died,

till even gentle Bacchus, the greatest and the first
to tread the grapes, desert those vats that I have cursed—
full punishment for those who steal our girls away.
For even the best of wine, that is too much to pay.
Down with crops, at least until our girls return—
acorns our food, and water out of a clay urn.
Our forefathers lived so, and they had love as well;
they never dug neat furrows in which seeds neatly fell.
In those distant days lovers found Venus mild;
they took her pleasures freely where the sunlit valleys smiled,
no one peering and prying, no locked doors breaking the heart.
Is it wrong to revive such customs, to make a fresh start?

. . . .

and let the hairy bodies be clothed in animal skins.
What good is a splendid toga if the way of love is barred,
if she is kept invisible forever under guard?
Lead me from Rome to her. There is nothing I will not yield:
let me be beaten or chained; let her bid me till the field.

II, iv

HIC MIHI SERVITIUM VIDEO DOMINAMQUE PARATAM...

She waits, and with her, bondage;
my fathers' freedom, farewell!
Slavery, chains, are my fate now,
the tight-bound shackles of love
to chafe me, all unjustly.
My cruel girl holds the torch
to my flesh—I would turn to stone
on the cold hills to escape,
or turn to a wind-vexed cliff
for waves to hurl ships against.
Bleak days and bleaker nights,
no moment without new gall:
no help in song, or its god—
her hand is outstretched for gold.
Be off, Muse, aidless to lovers,
I would not make war-chants
nor sing of the sun, or the night-route
of the horses of the moon.[39]
My song must open one door;
if it fails, then, Muse, be gone!
Must I murder and steal for gifts
to pass that wept-at gate?
Must I rob the holy shrines?
Love's temple shall be the first,
for he prompts me thus, and makes
my mistress grasping. His first!
Must men seek emeralds, dye
sheepskin with colors from Tyre,
sell silk and Indian pearls?
These tempt the covetous;

these turn the key in the lock,
and set the dog at the threshold—
but come with your hands full:
doors open and no dog barks.
What god matched beauty with greed,
that setting with such a gem?
Source of men's angry tears,
he is held cheap and unhoused.
May the girl who demands her price
lose her wealth in fire and wind—
her house ablaze, and none
helping to quench the flames;
may she die with none to grieve
or say a prayer at her grave.
But a generous girl should live
a hundred years, and be mourned
by crowds around her pyre—
and yearly some white-haired faithful
bring flowers to that tomb,
and, leaving, say, *Sleep well;*
may earth be light where you lie.
But who hears truth and is warned?
I must cherish her as she wills,
must sell my father's house
and ticket its gods for sale.
Medea's brew, and Circe's,
all the Thessalian herbs,
even the slimy fluid
a mare gives off in heat—
all these let Nemesis mix
in my drink, and if she smiles
I swear I will swallow it down.

II, v

PHOEBE, FAVE: NOVUS INGREDITUR TUA TEMPLA SACERDOS...

Your blessing, Phoebus; a new priest enters your temple.
Be gracious, greet his coming with voice and lyre,
and when your fingers set the strings to sounding,
let it be loyalty that they inspire.
Come, be among us while we heap the altars,
your brow encircled with a wreath of bay—
comb your long hair, put on your treasured raiment,
O come, god bright and beautiful as the day!
Be as you were when you sang of Jove's triumph
with Saturn finally driven from the throne.[40]
Prophet, the priest who serves you[41] learns the meaning
of the notes of that bird to which the future is known.[42]
You guide the lots as they fall; you show the augur
what marks of the god to read in the entrails;
with you as master, the Sibyl's six-metered strophes[43]
have given us counsel whose wisdom never fails.
Now let Messalinus touch the books of the seeress[44]
and know the meaning of each mysterious phrase.
She spoke to Aeneas when he had brought Anchises
and their household gods from a homeland all ablaze,[45]
and sailed, looking back in grief, on his destined voyage,
not dreaming he carried with him the fate of Rome.
(Years later, Romulus built the walls of the city,
driving his rival-brother out of their home,[46]
when Jupiter's hill had a cluster of huts to crown it[47]
and herds of cattle browsed on the Palatine;
a milk-drenched Pan stood in the ash-tree's shelter,[48]
and Pales graced a rough-carved wooden shrine;
a pipe, its thin voice stilled,[49] from a branch might dangle,
the shepherd's pledge for favors a god would show—

with its range of reeds from the largest to the lesser,
joined by wax in an ever-dwindling row.
And between those hills, in that now-crowded quarter,[50]
was a lake whose shallow waters were sometimes stirred
by the boat that brought a pretty girl to her lover,
who counted his wealth in thriving flock and herd,
and would give her gifts to take at her returning—
a white ewe's lamb, or cheese from the fresh curd.)
"Jupiter grants Laurentum to you, Aeneas,
unwearying as your brother, the winged boy—[51]
here you may land at last your ships of exile
and find a home for the homeless gods of Troy.
You will be worshipped here when the hallowed waters
of the Numicus bear your body to rest;[52]
over those weary ships now Victory hovers;
her fickle favor will come when they're hardest-pressed.
I see the burning camp of the Rutulians;[53]
barbaric Turnus, I predict your fall.
I can envision Ascanius' Alba Longa,
Laurentum's fortress, and Lavinium's wall—
and her who will bear the twin sons of the war-god:[54]
Ilia, leaving the shrine without a sound
for the secret bed, her hair loosed from its ribbon,
the great god's armor flung upon the ground.
Graze on the seven hills while you may, oxen,
where the city none shall surpass will find its site.
Rome, your nation will rule the round world over,
wherever Ceres watches from heaven's height,
from the opening gates of dawn to those tossing waters
where Ocean washes the Sun-god's horses clean.[55]
Troy herself shall marvel at Troy's story—
that in this far land her laurels should still be green.
Believe the words of one who will die a virgin[56]
and who eats unharmed the leaf of the sacred bay."[57]

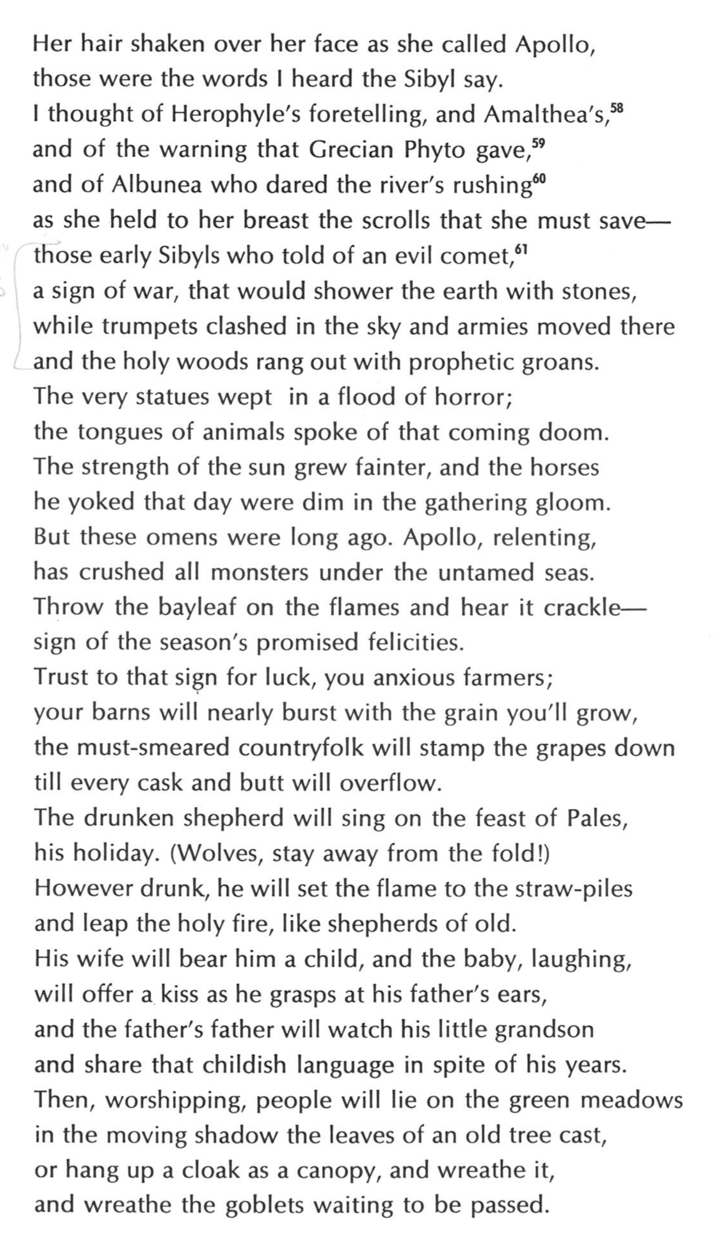

Her hair shaken over her face as she called Apollo,
those were the words I heard the Sibyl say.
I thought of Herophyle's foretelling, and Amalthea's,[58]
and of the warning that Grecian Phyto gave,[59]
and of Albunea who dared the river's rushing[60]
as she held to her breast the scrolls that she must save—
those early Sibyls who told of an evil comet,[61]
a sign of war, that would shower the earth with stones,
while trumpets clashed in the sky and armies moved there
and the holy woods rang out with prophetic groans.
The very statues wept in a flood of horror;
the tongues of animals spoke of that coming doom.
The strength of the sun grew fainter, and the horses
he yoked that day were dim in the gathering gloom.
But these omens were long ago. Apollo, relenting,
has crushed all monsters under the untamed seas.
Throw the bayleaf on the flames and hear it crackle—
sign of the season's promised felicities.
Trust to that sign for luck, you anxious farmers;
your barns will nearly burst with the grain you'll grow,
the must-smeared countryfolk will stamp the grapes down
till every cask and butt will overflow.
The drunken shepherd will sing on the feast of Pales,
his holiday. (Wolves, stay away from the fold!)
However drunk, he will set the flame to the straw-piles
and leap the holy fire, like shepherds of old.
His wife will bear him a child, and the baby, laughing,
will offer a kiss as he grasps at his father's ears,
and the father's father will watch his little grandson
and share that childish language in spite of his years.
Then, worshipping, people will lie on the green meadows
in the moving shadow the leaves of an old tree cast,
or hang up a cloak as a canopy, and wreathe it,
and wreathe the goblets waiting to be passed.

Each man will cut sods for the seats and sods for the table
and pile it high with wine and holiday fare;
and some lad who has drunk too much will curse his sweetheart—
curses he'll try to avert tomorrow with prayer,
swearing with tears that reason must have left him
to shout till she was both angry and alarmed.
Rid the earth of bows and arrows, Apollo,
so the god of love himself may roam unarmed.
It is not that I begrudge the fletchers their business—
but Cupid's arrows have struck too many hearts,
not least my own. I've hugged my grief for a year, now,
(it is in Love's pain that all his pleasure starts),
singing of Nemesis only, Nemesis always.
Without her my verse won't scan, the words come hard.
But you, my girl, watch out; the gods love poets;
I warn you, have respect for a sacred bard
singing of Messalinus, who drives before him
whole conquered cities—the victor, battle-scarred
and crowned with bay, while round him his bay-wreathed soldiers
deafen the crowd with their wild triumphal song.
Messalla will clap his hands in pride and affection
seeing his son ride by in a chariot there.
May your hair be uncut, Apollo, and your sister
a virgin forever,[62] if you will hear our prayer.

II, vi
CASTRA MACER SEQUITUR: TENERO QUID FIET AMORI?...

Macer's camp-bound—now what of gentle love?
must he go forth and shoulder Macer's arms?
will they be comrades on some endless march,
or on a troopship cross an angry sea?
Love, brand him: he deserts the lands of peace.
Recall the faithless truant to your ranks.
Or, if you pity soldiers, I'll be one,
a helmetful of water for my thirst—
I am ready. Venus farewell; farewell, my loves!
I'm strong, I love the piercing trumpet-call.
My words sound well—but my bravado fails;
the slamming of a door can strike me dumb—
that door I took an oath never to seek.
No use; my feet return of their own will.
I'd break your weapons if I could, fierce Love;
would, if I could, even put out your torch.
You stretch me on the rack; I curse myself
and all the gods; you leave me wild and spent.
I would have killed myself long since, but Hope
tempts me, and I believe her promises.
Why does she keep that spark alive in men?—
spurring them on to plant hard-fisted earth,
to net the fowl, to bait the hook for fish,
and comforting the slave, despite the chains
that clamp his legs—she bids him sing at his task.
She says that even Nemesis will be kind.
You cannot argue with a goddess, girl!
Soften your heart, remembering your sister
so early dead—relent, and let her sleep.
To me her spirit's blest; I offer her

gifts and garlands of flowers wet with tears.
She'll intercede for me; I'll tell my griefs
to her silence till it seems almost to speak.
She will not forgive you always. I beg of you
in her name, be merciful, lest you anger her
and she send you dreams in vengeance, horrible dreams,
or stand beside your bed, all bloody and bruised
as she was when we found her body on the shore,
fallen from window-ledge to lake below.
I'll say no more; I would not renew your tears:
I am not worth one cry of pain from you.
Sorrow should never redden those eloquent eyes.
You are good. It is Phryne, Phryne the bawd, that I fear.
With hidden poisons I know she plots my death;
though I hear your voice beyond the door, she'll say,
the liar, that no, her mistress is not at home;
or when I come to spend a promised night,
she'll swear that you're ill, or that the omens are wrong.
Then I could die, indeed, and, desperate,
ask myself whose arms are holding you.
Damn you, Phryne—your life should be hard to bear
if the gods heed half of what I say of you.

BOOK THREE

III, i

MARTIS ROMANI FESTAE VENERE KALENDAE...

It is the first of March, the feast of the war god—[63]
tradition calls it the opening of the year;
slaves rush with gifts from one house to another;
processions form and parade, go past, draw near.
Muses, tell me: what shall I bring to Neaera?
false or faithful, no matter; still most dear.
"Poetry for the beautiful, gold for the greedy—
she will delight in verses made for her ear.
But wrap the clean white roll in yellow parchment;
polish the page[64] as smooth as the polished phrase,
and at the top, like a border on the papyrus,
let your name be clearly printed to catch her gaze.
See that each roller's knobs are brightly painted—
her gift must be perfect in all of a hundred ways."
By the Pierian spring, by the shaded Castalian,[65]
Muses, to him you inspire grant what he prays:

go to her; bring, unchanged, my book, my treasure;
do not let those colors fade that please me so.
She will tell me whether she loves me still, or whether
less, or whether her heart would have me go.
But first offer the sort of generous greeting
she well deserves, and say—your voices low—
"This is the gift, Neaera chaste and lovely,
that brother who was once your husband[66] sends.
Accept it. Though you live as wife or sister,
you are the soul on which his life depends.
Better his wife—this hope he holds till Pluto
wills that the pale wave quench it,[67] and life ends."

III, ii

QUI PRIMUS CARAM IUVENI CARUMQUE PUELLAE...

Heartless he must have been who drove apart
for the first time the lover from his love;
and he too had a stone and not a heart
who, losing his beloved, still could live.
O I am weak, and my defenses few—
the stoutest spirit breaks under such a strain—
why should I blush when what I say is true?
I hate this fate-bedevilled life of mine.
When death has sucked my white bones marrow-dry,
hiding them under a cover of black ash—
your long hair loosed, Neaera, weeping, lie
where once the funeral fires took my flesh.
Your sorrow and your mother's both must share:
one for a husband and one for a son.
Call forth my ghost; invoke it with a prayer;
bring holy water; dip your fingers in;
wear black, unbelted; and those bones of mine,
last fragments of my body—gather them up
and sprinkle them the first time with old wine,
and then in brimming white milk let them steep,
and then with soft old linen wipe them clean
and make them ready for a marble tomb.
From lands that only the bravest men have seen,
from fabled isles, let all their treasure come—
poured forth, together with remembering tears.
Thus would I have my body laid to rest.
And carve a legend to outlast the years,
telling how love prevailed, but at what cost:
HERE LIES POOR LYGDAMUS, WHO GAVE HIS LIFE
IN LONGING FOR NEAERA, ONCE HIS WIFE.

III, iii

QUID PRODEST CAELUM VOTIS IMPLESSE, NEAERA...

Do the gods hear those vows of yours, Neaera,
or heed the incense, or the endless prayer?—
not that I walk forth from a marble mansion,
its owner, known and envied everywhere,
or that my oxen plow a thousand acres
and earth enrich the harvest of my farms;
but that I spend a long life's years beside you
and die within the circle of your arms
when the sun that has marked my span of time shall darken
and, stripped of all, I step on Charon's prow.
Much gold, like any other weight, is burden;
small good the fields a thousand oxen plow;
small good a house pillared with solid marble
from Phrygian or Laconian quarries' hoard,[68]
its rooms like sacred groves of wooden columns,
the cross-beams gilt, the rooms all marble-floored;
small good those great pearls of the Indian Ocean,
or fine wool dipped in Sidon's purple dyes,
or all things that men marvel at. There envy
lies hidden; men are tricked by what they prize.
Wealth never lightened heart or lessened trouble;
Fortune will move by Fortune's laws alone.
To one who has your love, poverty's nothing;
what's a royal treasure if you're not my own?
You will come back again, some snow-bright morning,
making that morning three and four times blest—
I know you will . . . And yet, if Love refuses
all that I've vowed him for that one request,
I shall not be appeased by power, or rivers
of Lydian gold, or all the opulent earth.

Others desire these. Leave me my cottage
and the dear wife I love; I know their worth.
Hear me, O Vesta, Saturn's daughter! hear me,
Cyprian Venus whose chariot is a shell![69]
If Destiny refuse, and those harsh sisters[70]
who spin the thread and weave our fate as well—
let livid Pluto, that lord of sluggish waters,
call me down to the desolate swamps of hell.

III, iv

DI MELIORA FERANT, NEC SINT MIHI SOMNIA VERA...

O gods, relent! make it no more than dream,
this evil vision I have wakened from.
Those prophets mouthing falsehood—strike them dumb!
why should it be deception that prevails?
Heaven sends true warnings, shows them in entrails
the Tuscan seer deciphers, the facts he tells.
But dreams, those random wanderers of the night—
deceptive terrors breed deceptive fright
(say they are false!) which men propitiate
with offerings of spelt and sputtering salt.
But whether dreams would warn the soul of guilt
or voice the lies of sleep instead, cry halt,
Lucina, to the horrors they have raised[71]
and let their victim's innocence be eased—
unless the gods refuse to be appeased
whom I by some impiety profane.
Night's chariot, by her four black horses drawn,
ended its journey in the seas of dawn,
yet sleep, friend of the sick, gave me no rest—
shunning a house so troubled and distressed.
Not till the god Apollo rose at last[72]
did peace come quietly to close my eyes
and show a figure, forehead crowned with bays,
poised on my threshold, luminous and wise.
No sight our ancestors have ever seen
was lovelier; no dream of mortal men:
the hair was long, the throat's line strong and clean;
the dews of Syria streamed from that dazzling head;
a radiance like the moon's around him spread;
the faintest rose his body's whiteness dyed—

delicate, like the blush of some young bride
first brought to her new home and led inside,
or lilies and amaranth that cannot fade
in wreaths, or apples, autumn's red on white.
His long robes hid the hallowed form from sight,
and the hem seemed to ripple round his feet.
At his left side a lyre hung, worked with skill
that made it gleam with gold and tortoise-shell,[73]
and while he sang, he plucked it with a quill.
But O the warning sung at that song's end!
"Gods love all poets," he said, "and such men find
Bacchus, Apollo, and each Muse a friend.
Yet those wise sisters and the god of wine—[74]
they lack the power to see the future plain.
Jove's gift of foresight is not theirs but mine.
To me, inevitable fate is clear.
Thus, hearing me, believe in what you hear
and learn how true Apollo's visions are.
No mother loves her daughter as you do
Neaera, and no husband is more true,
and for her good no man's more quick to pray.
No day goes by but that you fear her loss,
and when sleep wraps you in his robes of peace
her image breaks your rest and will not cease.
Though through your songs we know Neaera's name,
she takes another lover, spends with him
her nights, makes rules according to her whim,
is bored with virtue, would not be a wife
but takes delight in ruining your life,
dismissing all her treachery with a laugh—
the prototype of woman, who obeys
her nature, and, obedient, betrays.
Yet you may save her, for such minds as these
veer often. Stretch your hands to her and plead.

Our master Love will train us to his need;
we yield, or on our backs his lash is laid.
It is not told in mockery that I
served as Admetus' shepherd,[75] long ago,
and lost the will to play the lyre, or try
new harmonies for voice and strings to share—
but used an unstopped pipe, in my despair:
I, Jove-begotten, whom Latona bore!
You are a young man yet; you do not guess
love's deepest meaning, and will not, unless
you learn to bear the pain he brings to us.
Learn how a soft complaint can make her yield.
If in my sacred temples truth is told,
quote her the message that I now unfold:
Marked for each other, you must live as one;
delight in him, and take no other man."
He spoke, and suddenly my sleep was done—
I woke, weighed down with never-equalled woe.
Who'd guess that your whole soul was turned from me,
or that such evil in your heart could grow?
You are no daughter of the changeful seas,[76]
nor of Chimaera with her flame-filled jaws,
nor of that hound with three heads and three maws,[77]
its body by a troop of serpents spanned,
nor even of Scylla, by wild dogs girdled round.
No lioness bore you in some hideous land
like Scythia or the Syrtis all men fear—
yours is a home no ruffian comes near,
your mother the best of all her sex by far,
your father the most lovable of men.
Gods, change this dream to good, as night to dawn,
or bid the South Wind seize it and be gone!

III, v

VOS TENET, ETRUSCIS MANAT QUAE FONTIBUS UNDA...

Stay safely beside the stream of Etruscan waters—[78]
you cannot draw near to it in August's heat,
but now in the spring it is second only to Baiae
when the frost comes out of the ground and the air is sweet.
For me, Persephone warns, the dark approaches—
Goddess, why harm the innocent and young?
I have not tried to learn and to tell the secrets
of those holy rites no man may move among,[79]
nor have I ever been one who dealt in poisons
pounded from herbs or blended with the wine;
my hand has not set fire to sacred temples;
no crimes that shame the conscience trouble mine.
Never have I allowed rage and frustration
to urge my impious tongue to blasphemies.
My hair is still untouched by gray; my body
unbowed by age and its infirmities.
I was born in the year when the consuls died in battle—[80]
Hirtius and Pansa, after Caesar fell.
Why should you snatch green clusters from the grapevine,
or strip the branch before the fruit can swell?
Great Pluto, the loser when they cast for kingdoms,[81]
spare me, god of dark marshes and bleak lands;
put off the day when I must look on Lethe,
and the Blessed Fields,[82] and the dank Cimmerian sands;[83]
the days when years have made my lined cheek sallow
and I bore my listeners, talking of the past . . .
Mine may be all imaginary fevers—
yet would those for five days of weakness last?
Enjoy our Tuscan lakes, the naiad-haunted,[84]
their ripples parting lightly to the oar.

Love life, and do not let me be forgotten
if Fate decrees I share in it no more.
To the lords of death, black sheep be offered up,
and wine and white milk, mingled in a cup.

III, vi

CANDIDE LIBER ADEST: SIC SIT TIBI MYSTICA VITIS...

O splendid Bacchus, come, with your marvelous vine
as always, and with the ivy to wreathe your head!
Drive off my pain; give me your healing bowl
whose bounty has so often conquered Love.
Fill the goblets to overflowing, boy;
tilt the jar deeply, pouring that noble wine.
Heartbreak and all your heartless crew, be gone!
Welcome, Apollo, with your snowy birds,[85]
and welcome, friends—but promise to follow me;
once we begin, we'll have no laggards here.
If anyone fears to enter the lists with Bacchus,
may such a man find his sweetheart secretly false.
For it is Love who softens the heart, and brings
grief to the arrogant and an end to pride.
Armenian tigers and lionesses obey
that power of his that makes the untameable tame.
These things Love does, and more. But now we demand
another god's gifts. Who, pray, would drink water here?
Dionysus confronts us, our equal, our friend,
but we must pay court to him, and relish his wine—
there is no one he hates and will punish more than a prude.
It is wise to avoid a great god's anger, and drink.
Do you doubt his violence, the range of his wrath?
Remember mangled Pentheus, and be warned.[86]
Let us run no risk; if anyone shall test
the rage of a furious god, let it be that girl.
What have I said? I am mad. O winds and cloud,
sweep such a horrible wish to the ends of the earth.
Neaera, though even my name is gone from your heart,
I would only have you happy and fortunate.

No more of such thoughts. We must turn to our drinking now;
for the first time in a week, the skies are clear.
It is hard to pretend, to make false joy seem real,
to give the broken heart a smiling disguise.
But drunken words defile the lips of sorrow.
No use complaining—I must forget my cares;
Father Lenaeus does not pity grief.[87]
Long, long since, Ariadne, far from Crete,
mourned her betrayer on an alien shore.[88]
The great Catullus sang of you, Minos' daughter—[89]
how you were wed, abandoned, and cruelly used.
Friends, hear my warning: listen to all these tales
of suffering. You will spare yourselves much pain.
Do not be tricked when her arms shall hold you close
or her lying mouth murmur its wheedling words.
She'll swear by Juno, by Venus, by her own eyes—
no matter. There is never a shred of truth
in any word of hers. Since Jove absolves
lovers from oaths he'll let the winds bear off,
why should I beat the wall? She's like the rest.
Let's have no more such moaning, such despair . . .
And yet if I could spend night's quiet with you,
and with you make a vigil of our days—
my life, my light love, faithless through no fault
or faithlessness of mine, and still beloved . . .
Lord Bacchus loves the naiad.[90] Boy, bring wine.
You're slow. Now pour the Marcian water in.[91]
If, fickle and deceitful, she has fled
this table and its pleasures for new love,
shall I sigh out my heart the whole night long?
Here, pour the wine, and see that no drop spills.
Time wastes. Before it withers, set the wreath
here on my hair fragrant with Syrian nard.

III, vii — IV, i
PANEGYRICUS MESSALLAE
TE, MESSALLA, CANAM, QUAMQUAM TUA COGNITA VIRTUS...

I who must stand abashed before your fame
would praise you as my feeble powers permit.
Let me begin, and by beginning show
awareness of those honors due to you—
honors my talent cannot put in words:
only yourself could so recount those deeds
and not omit more than you chronicle.
Be generous to my efforts. The Sun-god
accepted Cretan tribute;[92] Bacchus found
Icarius' welcome warm—[93] to prove the tale,
Erigone and Maera shine as stars.
And Hercules, who would be made divine,
stayed with Molorchus at the vineyard's edge.[94]
A scattering of salt may please the gods
no less than would a bull with gilded horns.
This small beginning—may it gain your nod,
and from it may more fitting homage spring.

I cannot trace the structure of the world—
how Earth sank down in the enormous air
and how the Sea streamed over the round globe
and how, where clouds float away in space,
fiery Ether circumscribes the whole
and is in turn bound by the Firmament.
I offer you all that my Muse achieves,
whether her efforts reach your heights, or rise
(but how?) above them, or whether they fall—
and they must fall—below; your name redeems.
Born of a clan whose honors none can count,

you would not live upon your fathers' deeds,
nor gain your glory from their eulogies.
Yourself alone will make your own repute,
bequeathing greater fame than you were left.
Under your name there's far too little space
to list your exploits—these need deathless books,
and for their writing all men will compete,
bringing their best of poetry or prose,
hoping for first place—would that I might win,
that such a history might bear my name!
O unsurpassed in forum and battlefield,
as soldier famed, as statesman famed no less,
like a true scale, loaded with equal weights,
which keeps the balance of its lift and fall,
bearing the same amount in either pan
and each pan quivering beneath its load—
the crowd turned screeching mob your quiet voice
alone subdues; your words alone can calm
an angry juror who must be appeased.
Pylos, the home of Nestor—Ithaca,
that little town hailed as Ulysses' realm—
neither can claim a man as great as you,
though Nestor lived on while Hyperion's son
turned the earth's seasons for three hundred years,[95]
and though Ulysses roamed undaunted all
the ends of Earth where Ocean closes in,
battled the Thracian bands and drove them back,[96]
held to his course despite the lotos-snare,[97]
and once on Aetna's cliff tricked Neptune's son[98]
with wine till he could blind the single eye.
He brought the winds of Aeolus through the sea;[99]
saw tribes whose lands a great cold river floods—
the Laestrygonians, King Antiphates;[100]
alone survived the cup that Circe filled,[101]

Apollo's daughter, whose dark knowledge made
men into beasts by spells and magic herbs.
He knew the misty black Cimmerian lands[102]
where no man's eyes have ever watched the dawn
or seen the sunset or the stars at night.
Invading hell, he learned how Pluto led
the sons of gods to set laws for the dead;[103]
from his swift ship he heard the Sirens' song;[104]
he sailed a strait with death at either hand—[105]
unterrified by Scylla's six-mouthed charge
when she stole out through dog-infested waves,
and by Charybdis, whom so few escape,
caught as she rises out of the abyss
or as she falls and leaves the channel bare.
He stole the pastured cattle of the Sun,[106]
Calypso's fields, and, too, Calypso's love,[107]
and wandered wretched through Phaeacian lands.[108]
Did he move through our own familiar world
or was he first on some new continent?
Great as he was, he lacked your eloquence.
And none excels you in the art of war—
placing a ditch that must protect the camp;
building *chevaux de frise* to stop attack,
choosing the place that earthworks will enclose
where springs gush out sweet water, easily reached
by our men, but for others a steep climb.
You know how rivalry keeps men alert—
who best can shoot an arrow, drive a stake,
or slash a pathway clear with his short pike;
whose firm hand can hold back a lively horse
with a tight bit, or loose a slow beast's rein;
or who, in turn, can gallop a straight run
and make his mount wheel suddenly around;
whose shield can guard his right side as his left,

wherever the heavy spearhead may attack;
whose aim is most unerring with the sling.
And when the signal's given for the fight
and the opposing lines rush forth, their standards high,
you range the battle, see the whole design;
order the troops to form into a square
so that the dressed line runs with level front,
or split the army into equal parts,
each one sent forth to charge its opposite
and, after double hazard, doubly win.
These are not unproved praises that I sing—
your victories show their truth. As witness call
the courage of the lost Iapydians;[109]
the men who ambushed us among the Alps;[110]
the poor son of Arupium's fields,[111] so old
that tales of Nestor's age seem credible—
a man who sees a hundred ripening years
and himself hearty still, for without help
he still can get astride a frisky horse
and master it, his grip firm on the reins.
You were commander when that Gallic chief,
till then unconquered, bent beneath our chains.[112]
Nor does all this content you. What's to come
is greater than the past—I have read the signs;
Melampus could not leave me more convinced.[113]
You had put on the consul's purple robe[114]
at the first dawning of the fruitful year,
when, brighter than his wont, the Sun rose up
out of the waves, and the winds held their breath,
halting their warfare, and the rivers stopped.
Even the sea stood still, its waves becalmed,
and no bird flashed across the airs of heaven;
no savage beast that prowls the woodland bush
moved but gave humble silence to your prayers.

And Jove sped in his chariot to your side,
leaving Olympus, neighbor to the sky,
and bent his whole mind to your orison,
nodding that head that never utters lies.
Over the incense rose the altar fire.
The gods have summoned you. Begin! Press on!
Lesser men's triumphs—such are not for you.
The Gauls across our frontiers shall not stop
your progress, nor the wider lands of Spain;
nor yet Cyrene, which the Cretans held,
lands which the Nile, the royal Choaspes, feed,
nor that wild Gyndes which left Cyrus parched,[115]
nor Oroatis on the Araccan plain,
nor that Araxis which Tamyris made
her kingdom's limit, nor the Paedean,
where cannibals still make their hideous meal—
not all these far lands, distant as the Sun,
Scythia of the Don, the Danube's Thrace.

And how much more to tell! No race would dare
resist, through all the Ocean-circled Earth;
the still-unconquered Briton waits your rule
as the Earth's other part, past the Sun's path.
For the Earth rests upon the cradling air,
the whole globe made up of five different parts:
two of them wastelands of unending cold
where the ground never sees the light of day
and rivers freeze before they set their course,
thickened to ice and weighted down with snow
toward which the Sun-god never turns his face.
The central parts know nothing but his heat,
greater in summer, when he's nearest them,
and little less when he cuts short the day.
There the Earth's surface is not ridged by plows,

fields bear no corn, there is no pasturage.
No god of harvest ever tends that land,
whose empty deserts feed no animal.
Between it and the icy regions lie
two pleasant zones on either side the world—
made similar and controlled by those extremes
which when they meet must lose intensity.
And thus we have our gently-turning year;
thus we can tame the bull to bear the yoke,
can train the vine that climbs the lofty bough,
can harvest every fall the fields' ripe fruit.
Iron can plow the earth and bronze the sea,
and from the plains our high-walled cities rise.
So, when your deeds have gained their triumph, you
will win the name of master in both worlds.
What justice can I do to such repute,
although Apollo's self dictate my words?
Let Rufus Valgius—of all men today
closest to Homer—undertake the task.
My own work never ends in indolent ease—
Fortune will offer me, at best, a frown,
though once great wealth was mine, and a great house,
and yellow-furrowed land that poured its grain
into huge barns until they overflowed,
and crowds of cattle browsing on the hills—
enough for me, too much for thief and wolf.
Only the sense of loss remains, renewed
whenever grief recalls those lost delights.
Yet, though there's worse to come, though I am stripped
of all that's left, my song is still of you—
nor shall devotion stop with song. For you
I'd risk my life on the swift-moving sea
even when stormy straits are churned by wind;
for you I'd face alone an army's charge,

or give this worthless flesh to Aetna's flame.
All that I am or have is yours. If you
give me a kindly thought, however brief,
all the world's wealth would be of less import,
even the power to write as Homer wrote.
But if you know my verse, even a phrase,
and murmur it, nothing can stop my voice
in praise of you. When I am buried dust,
whether the day comes soon that marks my end
or whether death is slow, whether my soul
enters the body of a horse well-trained
to race the rough course, or becomes a bull,
pride of the slow herd, or a bird, perhaps,
winging its way through clear air—none the less,
when later ages make me man again,
what should my subject still be, then, but you?

III, viii

DE SULPICIA
SULPICIA EST TIBI CULTA TUIS, MARS MAGNE, KALENDIS...

Mars, great Mars, Sulpicia would celebrate your kalends[116]—
descend in your wisdom now from above, great god, to see her.
Venus will not resent it[117]—but have a care lest this beauty
make even you, the war-lover, drop your weapon in wonder.
Within her eyes will Love, a god no less violent, kindle
his double torches[118] when he would bring the gods under his power.
Her every motion is music itself, and close on her footsteps,
wherever they wander, follows a natural elegance.
Let her slip the bands from her hair—she could not be lovelier;
Let her bind and coil it again—she deserves no less our worship.
Clad in a purple gown, she will set your heart to burning,
nor will the flame die if her robe is white as a Vestal Virgin's.
Thus the god of the seasons may wear a thousand garments,[119]
each with an equal grace, there on the heights of Olympus.
Only for her that soft wool brought from distant Phoenicia
and dipped twice over in dyes more precious than any metal;
only for her whatever treasures the rich Arabian
reaps from that fabled land whose very fields are fragrant;
only for her those pearls born of the Red Sea waters—
pearls that dark-skinned men in the East, in India, dive for.
Sing of her beauty, O nine Muses, upon this feast-day;
Apollo, play on that tortoise-shell lyre a hymn to her beauty.
Year after year may she serve as our festival's reason:
no other girl in the land will give us more cause for song.

I, ix — IV, iii

PARCE MEO IUVENI, SEU QUIS BONA PASCUA CAMPI...

Boar whom he hunts in pastures of the plain
or on deep-shadowed mountains—spare my love,
O do not whet your hard tusks for defense!
Venus, protect him, keep him safe for me—
but no, she lures him from me to the chase.
Death to the dogs, a blight upon the woods!
What madness drives hands fit for better deeds
to ring the prey with nets on wooded slopes?
what joy to creep into the lairs of beasts
and let the thorn and bramble tear your legs?
And yet, Cerinthus, if you let me come,
I'll drag those twisted nets up hill down dale,
follow the tracks of the swift deer, and slip
the iron chain that holds the frantic hounds.
O I would love the forest, were I sure
that we might lie within it, near those nets:
then the wild boar might paw them and go free,
his hunters tangled in a subtler snare.
But without me, no loving. Keep the law
Diana sets, whose lovers must be chaste;
and should some other She usurp my place,
may she be torn to pieces by wild beasts.
Since it's your father's pleasure, let him hunt;
come back and take your pleasures in my arms.

III, x — IV, iv

HUC ADES ET TENERAE MORBOS EXPELLE PUELLAE...

Come near, Apollo, come and make me well—
heal me, Apollo of the flowing hair;
hear me and hasten; you will not regret
saving, by your hand's deftness, this fair maid.
And do not let her body waste away,
or lose its healthy color, or its strength.
O, may all evil, all the things we dread,
some cleansing river carry out to sea.
Be near me, holy presence; bring your songs
and all your delicacies that soothe the sick.
Lighten his hell who fears that I may die
and offers for my sake unending prayers—
though from that hell he utter blasphemies
against the gods who watch my suffering.
Cerinthus, do not fear; lovers are safe—
only be faithful; then I cannot die.
No reason now for weeping; save your tears
for some dark day when I am hard to please.
Now I think only of you, am wholly yours,
shun, for your sake, that crowd of confidantes.
Phoebus, be kind; all honor to that art
which, saving one from death, will rescue two.
Think of your pleasures when you see us try
each to outdo the offerings at your shrine!
All of Olympus, then, will call you blest
And envy you those life-restoring hands.

III, xi — IV, v

QUI MIHI TE, CERINTHE, DIES DEDIT, HIC MIHI SANCTUS...

The day that made you live for me, my love,
is henceforth hallowed, and my holiest fete.
When you were born, the Fates proclaimed aloud
you would be king and womankind your slaves.
More than the rest, I burn, but would rejoice
could your heart kindle, caught by that same fire.
I pray my love be yours—pray by your eyes,
our stolen hours, and your guardian-soul—
and bring that spirit incense now, and beg
that when you think of me your pulses rouse.
And if you sigh now for some other love?
Then, Venus, then forsake that faithless shrine!
Yet do not be unjust—let us be bound
in equal servitude, or set me free.
Had I my choice, I'd choose the double yoke—
light, but too strong even for time to break.
He too would ask this, but he lacks the words,
and so must hide his longing in his heart.
God of his birthday, since the gods know all,
give us your blessing, though his prayer is mute.

III, xii — IV, vi

NATALIS JUNO, SANCTOS CAPE TURIS ACERVOS...

Juno of birthdays[120], holy incense heaped
in her soft hands the maiden offers you.
Fresh-bathed, fresh-robed, rejoicing, she is yours,
and at your altar stands for all to see.
You know, great goddess, why she wears her best,
you know the secret one whom she would please.
Watch over them, that they need never part;
forge for him bonds as lasting as her own.
What better match?—each one of them well worth
all the devotion, all the fervor, pledged.
And let no guardian blunder on their trysts;
teach love a thousand ways to keep him blind.
Be gracious, and in shining robes come forth;
accept thrice-offered cake, thrice-offered wine.
Her mother tells her now for what to pray;
heedless, she makes her own, her silent choice:
a flame burns in her as the altars burn—
if this is madness, she would not be sane.
Juno, be kind, that, when a new year comes,
this same sustaining love may bless their prayers.

III, xiii — IV, vii

SULPICIAE ELEGIDIA

TANDEM VENIT AMOR, QUALEM TEXISSE PUDORI...

This day has brought a love
it would shame me to conceal—
won by song and prayer
Venus gives him to my arms
and all that she promised comes true.
Let my love be told by the loveless,
my letters go unsealed
and any read them who will.
If I sin, I glory in sinning:
I will not wear virtue's mask—
the world shall know we have met
and are worthy, one of the other.

III, xiv — IV, viii

SULPICIAE ELEGIDIA INVISUS NATALIS ADEST, QUI RURE MOLESTO...

How can I celebrate
this dismal birthday, tell me,
when I must be without
my love and far from Rome?
What can the country offer
a girl shut in a farmhouse
staring at fields and a chilly
stream? Was I born for this?
Too-kind Messalla, don't heed me;
journeys set their own time.
Reluctant victim, not mistress,
of my fate, I go, dear cousin—
leaving my heart and soul
behind me here at home.

III, xv — IV, ix

SULPICIAE ELEGIDIA SCIS ITER EX ANIMO SUBLATUM TRISTE PUELLAE?...

Darling, have you heard?—
all my qualms were groundless:
I shall be here for my birthday,
I shall be here in Rome.
Let that day, so nearly missed,
be marked by us together,
the anniversary shared
that chance has thrown our way.

III, xvi — IV, x

SULPICIAE ELEGIDIA
GRATUM EST, SECURUS MULTUM QUOD IAM TIBI DE ME...

Cheering it is to learn
what you allow yourself,
that I may fall
not wholly undeceived.
Your wench with her wool-baskets,
your own wardrobe—
these you choose over
Sulpicia, Servius' daughter!
What stirs my friends
is fear that I may surrender
to one beneath contempt.

III, xvii — IV, xi
SULPICIAE ELEGIDIA
ESTNE TIBI, CERINTHE, TUAE PIA CURA PUELLAE...

Can you spare a thought for your girl
who lies here parched with fever?
do you pray for my life? without
your prayers I would have it over.
Why should I struggle to live
if my death will not move my lover?

III, xviii — IV, xii

SULPICIAE ELEGIDIA
NE TIBI SIM, MEA LUX, AEQUE IAM FERVIDA CURA...

I would not deserve that love
I had in a happier time
if ever in all my life
I could be charged with a crime
repented more than the one
now I am guilty of—
who left you last night alone,
lest I make too clear my love.

III, xix — IV, xiii

INCERTI AUCTORIS
NULLA TUUM NOBIS
SUBDUCET FEMINA LECTUM...

No other will lie on this bed that we have shared, I promise—
that was the pledge we made when we fell in love.
Where would I find your equal, tell me? In all this city
there is no woman but you I would look at twice.
If it were only to my eyes that you seem so lovely!
Let other men be blind to you—then I am safe;
let them have everything that they prize; I shall not envy.
Wisdom hides what it cherishes deep in its heart.
Having you, I would live hidden away in a forest
where no footsteps but ours would trace a path.
You are my rest, my solace, my sustenance; in darkness
my light, in solitude my companionship.
Though the gods contrived to send me a mistress straight from
  Olympus,
she would be sent in vain; I would turn away.
This I swear to you in the holy name of Juno,
whom I, like you, hold high above other gods.
But what have I said? with these words I have lost my advantage;
your fear was my strength—I must have been mad when I spoke.
Now I have shown my weakness, how you can torment me!
will I never hold my mischief-making tongue?
Do whatever you choose; I shall be yours forever,
shall not even try to escape the familiar bonds—
no, I shall sit in my chains at the sacred altar of Venus,
who will punish the perjured and answer the lover's prayer.

III, xx — IV, xiv

INCERTI AUCTORIS
RUMOR AIT CREBRO
NOSTRAM PECCARE PUELLAM...

They say that my girl is unfaithful, over and over—
I would rather be struck deaf than hear those words.
How can such whispers bring me less than heartbreak?
Why must you torture me, Rumor? I beg you, be silent.

NOTES

1. *the first fruit . . . goes to the guardian god.* The reference is to no specific deity and is apparently intentionally indefinite on Tibullus' part.
2. *prying and Argus-eyed.* Juno changed Io into a heifer in revenge for her illicit affair with Jupiter. She also sent the monster Argus to watch her. Since he had many eyes, he performed this task very efficiently.
3. *Venus is born of blood and of the ocean.* Venus was born from the foam of the sea. When angered she was proverbially cruel (of blood).
4. *baring their own soft breasts and spitting there.* An apotropaic reaction occasioned by the old man's folly.
5. *Three times she lifted the lots from the boy's hands.* The lots were drawn three times for luck, and in the ancient world children were often considered to have powers of divination.
6. *to start on Saturn's day.* Saturn's day *(Saturni dies)* was the ancestor of the modern Saturday. Here the reference is to the Jewish Sabbath, when it was considered unlucky to initiate any important undertaking.
7. *O Isis whom Delia worships.* Isis was an Egyptian goddess of fertility whose mystery cult was well entrenched in Rome by Tibullus' day. Her worship involved a complicated ritual.
8. *in the days of Saturn's kingship.* That is, during the Golden Age.
9. *Snakes hiss on the head of the watchdog.* The watchdog is the never sleeping Cerberus who guarded the entrance to the Lower World. He was more of a dragon than a dog, with snakes growing out of his body. He is usually depicted in art as having three heads.
10. *Dawn, driving your rosy horses.* Here Tibullus invokes Aurora, the dawn-goddess. She drives a chariot pulled by two horses through the sky. One of her stock epithets in Greek epic is "rosy-fingered."
11. *by his decree no lover need keep the pledge.* The reference is to the story of Jupiter and Io. After Io was turned into a heifer, Jupiter swore to Juno that he did not have an affair with her. All is fair in love and war.
12. *though he has sworn upon Dictynna's arrows . . . or Minerva's hair.* Diana and Minerva would be least likely to pardon a lover since they were virgin goddesses. Diana is associated with bow and arrows and

quiver since she was the goddess of the hunt. Minerva was exceptionally proud of her hair. See DICTYNNA in Glossary.

13. *marked with the colored bow that threatens rain.* For the ancients the rainbow was a portent of an approaching thunderstorm.
14. *the purple lock of Nisus.* Nisus, king of the Megara, had a purple lock. It was believed that he would not die until the lock was cut. Out of love for Minos, king of Crete, his daughter Scylla did cut it. Nisus died and Megara fell.
15. *Pelops' shoulder of ivory.* Tantalus, Pelops' father, killed his son and served his flesh to the gods. Jupiter brought him back to life and gave him an ivory shoulder in place of the one eaten by Ceres.
16. *slash himself while the Phrygian music shrills.* The cult of Cybele (see CYBELE in Glossary) was highly orgiastic. Male celebrants often castrated themselves and were known as eunuchs. Phrygia was a center for Cybele's worship.
17. *the god would have me sing to Titius.* Attempts to identify this man have been unsuccessful. It has been suggested that the name is the Latin equivalent of "John Doe."
18. *riding a bridled dolphin to her prince.* Being a sea-nymph, Thetis rides a dolphin to Peleus, her mortal husband. Their son was the hero Achilles.
19. *she must serve the goddess where no man may fare.* The goddess is Bona Dea (Good Goddess). She was worshipped exclusively by women, and traditionally any man who violated her mysteries would be struck blind. Ceremonials in her honor were held at night.
20. *From the gods' mountain.* Mt. Olympus, situated on the border of Macedonia and Thessaly and the highest mountain in Greece, was considered the home of the gods.
21. *The Fates . . . intent on their spinning.* See FATES in Glossary.
22. *beyond the harbor town.* The reference is to ancient Narbo Martius, now Narbonne.
23. *that dove the Syrians worship.* The white doves of Syria were sacred to Astarte, Oriental equivalent of Venus.
24. *how Tyre . . . mastered the sea on which its towers look down.* The Phoenician island city of Tyre was famous for its trade and high buildings.
25. *What reason give that you have hidden your head.* The actual source of the Nile river was a much disputed topic in antiquity.
26. *The river-god and Osiris—theirs is a double altar. . . .* Jupiter Pluvius in his capacity of rain-giver is the river-god. Osiris was an Egyptian deity of fertility who was worshipped with Isis, his wife and sister. The bull Apis was his reincarnation on earth, and whenever an Apis died, the priests would shriek out hymns of grief. By "double altar"

Tibullus simply means that the Egyptians worship both Jupiter Pluvius and Osiris.

27. *Come to us, Spirit.* The Spirit is Messalla's "guardian angel."
28. *let him not be silent on that great work.* After the civil wars Augustus carried out a program of road repairs. To Messalla was assigned the overseeing of repairs of a portion of the *Via Latina* southeast of Rome.
29. *if the echoing bronze is left unstruck.* The allusion is to the practice of making a lot of noise during a lunar eclipse in order to frighten away its cause.
30. *Let the Fire-god shrivel my verses.* The reference is to Vulcan, god of fire.
31. *And now look for the liver marks the entrails show.* One way of divining the disposition of the gods was for the seers to examine the entrails of various animals.
32. *Bring me Falernum's smoky wine from the bin.* Sealed jars of wine were placed near a source of heat to improve the taste of the wine as well as to lend the containers an antique appearance. Falernian wine was a favorite with the Romans.
33. *and break the bands on the Chian jar.* Chios, a large island off the coast of Asia Minor, was famous for its wine.
34. *Night yokes her team.* Darkness comes about as Night drives her four-horsed chariot through the sky.
35. *the pearls that the great red sea of blessed India yields.* The reference is to the Persian Gulf.
36. *You tended Admetus' herds once.* In Greek mythology Apollo killed the Cyclops, forgers of Zeus' thunderbolts, to avenge the death of his son Asclepius at the hands of Zeus. By way of punishment Zeus forced Apollo to serve the mortal Admetus, king of Pherae in Thessaly, for a period of time as a herder.
37. *hair which had seemed to his stepmother so marvelously fair.* Apollo's stepmother was Juno, as she was the stepmother of all the illegitimate children sired by Jupiter.
38. *A man . . . may once have danced as a slave on gypsum-whitened feet.* When barbarian slaves were being sold their feet were whitened with chalk or gypsum.
39. *I would not make war-chants nor sing of the sun.* Tibullus means that he has no inclination to write epic in the Homeric sense (war-chants) or epic in the didactic sense (by writing of the sun and moon).
40. *when you sang of Jove's triumph with Saturn finally driven from the throne.* The reference is to Jupiter's wresting away power from his father Saturn, thereby becoming the new king of the gods.
41. *Prophet, the priest who serves you.* Apollo, having been addressed as the god of song at the beginning of the poem, is now addressed as god of prophecy.

42. *notes of that bird to which the future is known.* The reference is to no particular bird, but rather to the process of divination through interpreting the sounds of birds; more frequently their pattern of flight was observed.
43. *the Sibyl's six-metered strophes.* The Sibyl gave her oracular responses in dactylic hexameters.
44. *Now let Messalinus touch the books of the seeress.* The oracles of the Sibyl were collected in books which still existed in Tibullus' day and could be consulted.
45. *from a homeland all ablaze.* That is, from Troy. The story of the destruction of Troy is told in Book II of Vergil's *Aeneid.*
46. *driving his rival-brother out of their home.* The allusion is to Romulus' slaying of his brother Remus for leaping over the walls of early Rome.
47. *when Jupiter's hill had a cluster of huts to crown it.* The reference is to the Capitoline hill on which there was eventually built a temple to Jupiter Optimus Maximus (Jupiter the Best and Greatest). This temple was officially the capitol of Rome.
48. *a milk-drenched Pan stood in the ash-tree's shelter.* Milk was a regular offering to rustic divinities, and the ash-tree was sacred to Pan.
49. *a pipe, its thin voice stilled.* The reference is to the shepherd's reed-pipe, an invention of Pan. It was constructed of several reeds gradually decreasing in length and caliber. Shepherds would often offer their pipes in return for a favor from some god.
50. *in that now crowded quarter.* The reference is to the area known as the Velabrum, located between the Capitoline, Palatine, and Aventine hills. It was one of the busiest centers in Rome.
51. *unwearying as your brother, the wingèd boy.* That is, Cupid.
52. *You will be worshipped here when the hallowed waters of the Numicus bear your body to rest.* Aeneas died near the Numicus river and was worshipped as a patron deity of the immediate area.
53. *I see the burning camp of the Rutulians.* The Rutulians were a native people of Latium ruled by King Turnus. The Trojans and the Rutulians fought, but there is no tradition of the burning of the Rutulian camp. Perhaps the Sibyl refers here to Turnus' attempt to burn the Trojan ships. Aeneas finally killed Turnus.
54. *and her who will bear the twin sons of the war-god.* The allusion is to the birth of Romulus and Remus. While drawing water from a river, Rhea Silvia, the daughter of Numitor, a king of Alba Longa, was approached by Mars, god of war. Their offspring were the famous twins.
55. *where Ocean washes the Sun-god's horses clean.* According to Homeric tradition an ocean stream surrounded the world. At dawn the Sun and his horses rise from the eastern part of the stream, where

they are purified in the waters of Ocean. At evening they sink into the western part of the stream and again are purified in the life-giving waters.

56. *one who will die a virgin.* All the Sibyls were virgin prophetesses.
57. *who eats unharmed the leaf of the sacred bay.* Bay leaves were sacred to Apollo. It was thought that by chewing them one would become inspired.
58. *I thought of Herophyle's foretelling, and Amalthea's.* According to one tradition, the Sibyl Herophyle instructed Aeneas to sail westward until he arrived at a place where he and his followers would eat their tables, for at that place they were destined to reach an end of their journeys. They fulfilled the prophecy at Laurentum by eating what must have been the ancient prototype of the modern pizza or something of the sort. The crust was the table for the food placed upon it. According to Vergil, this prophecy was given to Aeneas by the harpy Celaeno. As for Amalthea, the allusion is obscure. According to one tradition, it was she who sold the Sibylline Books to Tarquinius Priscus, the fifth king of Rome. Perhaps she is to be identified with the Cumaean Sibyl.
59. *the warning that Grecian Phyto gave.* No satisfactory explanation of the allusion has been offered.
60. *Albunea who dared the river's rushing.* Albunea was a nymph of a sulphurous water rising at Tibur (modern Tivoli) and flowing into the Anio river. With the advent of the cult of the Sibyls into Italy Albunea became one. Here Tibullus alludes to a local legend according to which she swam the Anio, taking with her and thus saving certain sacred scrolls containing prophecies.
61. *those early Sibyls who told of an evil comet.* Comets were thought to portend serious disasters. Here the reference is to the so-called *Stella Crinita,* the star of Caesar which attended his death and the civil wars.
62. *your sister a virgin forever.* Apollo's sister was the virgin goddess Diana.
63. *the feast of the war god.* Mars had several major festivals in March. Here the reference is to the *Feriae Martis* held on March 1st; it traditionally opened the Roman New Year.
64. *polish the page.* The ancient book consisted of a scroll which was rolled up when not in use. The roughness of the two ends could be removed by polishing with a pumice stone.
65. *By the Pierian spring, by the shaded Castalian.* No special spring is meant by the "Pierian spring." Several springs in the area of Pieria in Macedonia were sacred to the Muses; Pieros was their father. The Castalian spring was on Mt. Parnassus.
66. *that brother who was once your husband.* Lygdamus and Neaera were either married or betrothed at one time. It is clear that they are now

estranged and that any affection between them is limited to a brotherly-sisterly sort.

67. *the pale wave quench it.* The reference is to the waters of the river Styx in the Lower World over which the dead crossed to enter Hades.
68. *solid marble from Phrygian or Laconian quarries' hoard.* Marble was to be found in Phrygia (modern Asia Minor), which was famous for its natural wealth. More significant were the deposits in Laconia, a district in the southeastern Peloponnese.
69. *Cyprian Venus whose chariot is a shell.* Venus had a major shrine on the island of Cyprus and is often referred to as the "Cyprian." Since she was born from the sea, it is logical that her chariot should be a shell.
70. *those harsh sisters.* The reference is to the Fates. See FATES in Glossary.
71. *cry halt, Lucina, to the horrors they have raised.* Lucina properly is an epithet of Juno in her capacity of goddess of childbirth, for it is she who causes a child to see the light of day (Lat. *lucina* = light-bearing). Here Lygdamus has had a bad dream involving Neaera, and since Juno was also connected with the sexual life of women, the poet invokes her to put an end to such dreams.
72. *Not till the god Apollo rose at last.* The reference is to Apollo as the Sun-god.
73. *with gold and tortoise-shell.* Apollo made the first lyre from the shell of a tortoise.
74. *those wise sisters and the god of wine.* That is, the Muses and Bacchus.
75. *I served as Admetus' shepherd.* See note 36.
76. *You are no daughter of the changeful seas.* That is, Neaera is not a sea-monster.
77. *hound with three heads and three maws.* The reference is to Cerberus. See note 9.
78. *stream of Etruscan waters.* The reference is to the Tiber river, which had its source in Etruria.
79. *those holy rites no man may move among.* The reference is to the rites of Bona Dea (Good Goddess); see note 19.
80. *in the year when the consuls died in battle.* That is, in 43 B.C. After the assassination of Julius Caesar, Antony besieged the town of Mutina in Cisalpine Gaul. The two consuls, Aulus Hirtius and Gaius Vibius Pansa, died there in battle.
81. *Pluto, the loser when they cast for kingdoms.* The allusion is to the casting of lots whereby the brothers Jupiter, Neptune, and Pluto determined their spheres of influence. Jupiter won the land, Neptune the water, and Pluto the Lower World.
82. *the Blessed Fields.* That is, the Elysian Fields; see Glossary.
83. *the dank Cimmerian sands.* The Cimmerians were supposed to have

lived in caves between Baiae and Cumae in southern Italy. Here the reference is simply to the Lower World.

84. *Tuscan lakes, the naiad-haunted.* See NAIAD in Glossary.
85. *Welcome, Apollo, with your snow birds.* Since swans were celebrated for their singing, they were consecrated to Apollo in his capacity as patron deity of music.
86. *Remember mangled Pentheus, and be warned.* Pentheus was a king of Thebes who made the mistake of treating the rites of Bacchus with contempt. He was torn to pieces by a group of frenzied female devotees of Bacchus led by his own mother, Agave.
87. *Father Lenaeus does not pity grief.* Lenaeus was another name for Bacchus, god of wine.
88. *Ariadne . . . mourned her betrayer on an alien shore.* Ariadne was the daughter of Minos, king of Crete. With her help Theseus was able to kill the Minotaur and escape from the Labyrinth. Theseus took Ariadne with him when he fled from Crete, but abandoned her on the island of Naxos.
89. *The great Catullus sang of you, Minos' daughter.* The story of Ariadne and Theseus is told in the sixty-fourth poem of Catullus.
90. *Lord Bacchus loves the naiad.* Properly a naiad is a nymph of a fountain or spring. Here the allusion is simply to the common practice among the ancients of mixing their wine with water.
91. *Now pour the Marcian water in.* The praetor Quintus Marcius Rex built an aqueduct in 144 B.C. The water which it supplied was famous for its purity.
92. *The Sun-god accepted Cretan tribute.* The allusion is to the foundation of Apollo's cult at Delphi. The first priests of the new cult were Cretan sailors. Delphi is so named because Apollo first appeared to the sailors in the form of a dolphin (Greek *delphis* = dolphin).
93. *Bacchus found Icarius' welcome warm.* Bacchus was once hospitably received by the Athenian Icarius and his daughter Erigone. In return, Icarius learned the art of making wine. After Icarius was killed by certain shepherds whom he had made drunk, his dog Maera led Erigone to his corpse. The three were transformed into constellations by Bacchus.
94. *Hercules . . . stayed with Molorchus at the vineyard's edge.* When Hercules went to kill the Nemean lion he was entertained by Molorchus, a poor vineyard keeper at Cleonae.
95. *Nestor lived on while Hyperion's son turned the earth's seasons for three hundred years.* The allusion is to the extreme old age of Nestor, king of Pylon. The titan Hyperion was the father of the Sun, and Nestor was supposed to have lived over a hundred years.
96. *Ulysses . . . battled the Thracian bands and drove them back.* The

reference is to Ulysses' encounter with the Cicones, a people of Thrace, shortly after he left Troy.

97. *Ulysses . . . held to his course despite the lotos-snare.* In his wanderings Ulysses visiting the land of the Lotos-eaters. Anyone who ate the flower forgot his own country and desired to live in Lotos-land; hence the snare.
98. *Ulysses . . . once on Aetna's cliff tricked Neptune's son.* The allusion is to Ulysses' blinding of the Cyclops Polyphemus, son of Neptune, after he had gotten him drunk. According to the tradition here, this happened in Sicily.
99. *He brought the winds of Aeolus through the sea.* Aeolia was the home of Aeolus, ruler of the winds. He gave Ulysses a sack of all the winds except the one which would bring him home to Ithaca.
100. *the Laestrygonians, King Antiphates.* Ulysses barely escaped with his ship and crew after he visited the land of the Laestrygonians, a race of cannibalistic giants. Their king was Antiphates.
101. *alone survived the cup that Circe filled.* From Laestrygonia Ulysses sailed to Aeaea, home of Circe, the goddess-sorceress. She changed Ulysses' men into swine through a magic potion, but Ulysses himself was able to resist her spells.
102. *He knew the misty black Cimmerian lands.* That is, Ulysses went to the Lower World at the suggestion of Circe in order to consult with the seer Tiresias.
103. *Pluto led the sons of gods to set laws for the dead.* The allusion is to the three judges of the Lower World: Minos, Rhadamanthus, and Aeacus. All were sons of Jupiter.
104. *he heard the Sirens' song.* The Sirens were enchantresses who were half bird and half woman. No mortal could resist their song, and they killed those sailors whom they lured to their island. Ulysses stuffed the ears of his crew with wax so that they would not fall victims. He himself did hear the Sirens' song, but only after he had himself tied to his ship's mast.
105. *he sailed a strait with death at either hand.* That is, Ulysses sailed through the Straits of Messina with Scylla on one side and Charybdis on the other. See SCYLLA and CHARYBDIS in Glossary.
106. *He stole the pastured cattle of the Sun.* Ulysses then came to the island where the cattle of the Sun pastured. He and his crew ate the cattle when their provisions ran short. In revenge the Sun-god destroyed Ulysses' ship and Ulysses alone survived.
107. *Calypso's fields, and, too, Calypso's love.* Calypso was a nymph who lived on the island of Ogygia. She received Ulysses after he was shipwrecked by the Sun-god. She fell in love with her guest and was finally forced to let him go after he had spent seven years with her.
108. *wandered wretched through Phaeacian lands.* After leaving Ogygia

Ulysses lost the new ship which he had built there and swam ashore at Scheria, the land of the Phaeacians. For a while he wandered in bewilderment, but was finally received by King Alcinous and his daughter Nausicaa. Alcinous sent Ulysses home after entertaining him lavishly.

109. *the courage of the lost Iapydians.* The Iapydians were a people of northern Illyria (roughly modern Yugoslavia) who were subjugated after they revolted in 36 B.C.
110. *men who ambushed us among the Alps.* The revolt of the Iapydians was followed by that of the Pannonians, a people who lived between the Danube and the eastern Alps.
111. *the poor son of Arupium's fields.* The reference is simply to the soldiers of Arupium, a town in Iapydia. The land was poor, but even the old men were able to fight in war.
112. *that Gallic chief . . . bent beneath our chains.* The reference is to the chieftain Domator. Gallic tribes had mixed with the native Illyrians.
113. *Melampus could not leave me more convinced.* Melampus, son of Amythaon, was a famous prophet and missionary of Bacchus.
114. *You had put on the consul's purple robe.* That is, the *toga praetexta.* Messalla was consul in 31 B.C.
115. *that wild Gyndes which left Cyrus parched.* While Cyrus I, king of Persia, was marching against Babylon, one of his sacred white horses drowned in the Gyndes river. Cyrus was so furious with the river that he had his army split it into 360 separate channels.
116. *great Mars, Sulpicia would celebrate your kalends.* The first day of any Roman month was known as the kalends, and March was the month of Mars. Here the allusion is to the *Matronalia,* a festival of Juno held on March 1st. At that time women dressed in festive attire and received gifts from their husbands or lovers.
117. *Venus will not resent it.* The allusion is to the love affair between Mars and Venus.
118. *kindle his double torches.* The torches are merely his two eyes.
119. *Thus the god of the seasons may wear a thousand garments.* Vertumnus was the Roman god of the seasons and was associated with the fruits of the earth. He could assume any attractive form he wished.
120. *Juno of birthdays.* The "guardian angel" of a man was known as his *genius* and that of a woman as her *Juno.*

NAME AND PLACE GLOSSARY

Admetus. *King of Pherae in Thessaly. The god Apollo was forced to serve him as a shepherd. (See note 36.)*

Aegean. *The sea between Greece and Asia Minor.*

Aeneas. *Son of the mortal Anchises and the goddess Venus and hero of Vergil's* Aeneid. *After the fall of Troy he sailed to Italy, where he laid the foundations of what would eventually become the Roman state.*

Aetna. *A volcano in Sicily.*

Alba Longa. *A colony traditionally founded by Ascanius, son of Aeneas; located twelve miles southeast of Rome. Now Castel Gandolfo.*

Albunea. *The Sibyl of Tibur. (See note 60 and* Sibyl.)

Amalthea. *The Sibyl who may have sold the Sibylline Books to Tarquinius Priscus. (See* Sibyl.)

Anchises. *Father of the Trojan hero Aeneas, with whom he sailed westward after the fall of Troy.*

Anio. *A tributory of the Tiber river; now the Teverone.*

Antiphates. *The king of the cannibalistic Laestrygonians, a people visited by Ulysses in the course of his wanderings. (See* Laestrygonia.)

Apollo. *A Greek god, son of Zeus and Leto (Jupiter and Latona) and brother of Artemis (Diana); born on the island of Delos. He invented the lyre and was the patron god of the arts; also a god of prophecy and of the sun.*

Aquitania. *The region between the Garonne river, the Pyrenees, and the Bay of Biscay; the area of modern Gascony. Messalla, having subjugated the Aquitanians, was given a triumph in 27 B.C.*

Aracca. *A coastal plain area in Persia bordering on the Persian Gulf.*

Araxes. *A river in Armenia; now frequently called the Aras.*

Argus. *A many-eyed monster sent by Juno to watch Io after she had been changed into an heifer. (See note 2.)*

Ariadne. *Daughter of Minos and princess of Crete. She made it possible for Theseus to slay the Minotaur, and the two fled from Crete together. Theseus eventually deserted her on the island of Naxos.*

Arupium. *A town in Iapydia. (See* Iapydia.)

Ascanius. *Son of Aeneas and founder of Alba Longa; also known as Iulus and thereby founder of the Julian clan.*

Atax. *A small river in southern France; now called the Aude.*

Bacchus. *The god of wine. Also called Liber, Lenaeus, and Lyaeus; the Greek Dionysus.*

Baiae. *A town in the area of the Bay of Naples; famous as a fashionable resort.*

Bellona. *A Cappadocian goddess whose worship was orgiastic and ecstatic. Also the name of the Roman war-goddess.*

Calypso. *A nymph of the island of Ogygia who fell in love with Ulysses when he landed there in the course of his wanderings. She detained him for seven years.*

Campania. *The region of Italy surrounding Naples; noted for its luxuriousness.*

Castalia. *A fountain on Mt. Parnassus which was sacred to Apollo and the Muses.*

Catullus. The *renowned Roman lyric poet, Gaius Valerius Catullus (ca. 84-54 B.C.).*

Cerberus. *The three-headed watchdog of the Lower World.*

Ceres. *Goddess of the fruits of the earth, especially associated with the cultivation of wheat. She was the mother of Proserpine (Persephone); the Greek* Demeter.

Cerinthus. *The man whom the poetess Sulpicia loved.*

Charon. *The ferryman who transported the dead across the river Styx to Hades.*

Charybdis. *A dangerous whirlpool or maelstrom at the Straits of Messina. It would suck in the surrounding water and belch it forth three times a day. Charybdis was usually paired with Scylla. (See* Scylla.)

Chimaera. *A fire-breathing monster which was partly lion, serpent, and she-goat.*

Chios. *An island in the Aegean Sea off the coast of Asia Minor; famous for its wine.*

Choaspes. *A river in the Persian province of Susiana. The Persian kings drank from its celebrated pure waters; now frequently called the Kerrah.*

Cilicia. *A region of southern Asia Minor.*

Cimmerians. *Properly a legendary race of people who lived in caves in southern Italy; frequently their abode is identified with the Lower World.*

Circe. *A goddess-sorceress who lived on the island of Aeaea and who was famous for her magical powers. In the* Odyssey *she turns* Odysseus' *(Ulysses') men into swine.*

Cornutus. *A friend of Tibullus; perhaps to be identified with* Cerinthus. *(See* Cerinthus.)

Cos. *One of the Sporades islands in the Aegean Sea; famous for its silk.*

Cumae. *A very old Greek colony not far from Naples and site of the oracular cavern of the Sibyl. (See* Sibyl.) *It was also famous for the quality of its handsome but inexpensive pottery.*

Cybele. *The mother-goddess of Anatolia, often referred to as* magna mater *(Great Mother). She was worshipped along with her young lover Attis, a god of vegetation. Her rites were officially introduced into Rome at the end of the third century B.C. Her worship was highly orgiastic and ecstatic.*

Cydnus. *A river in Cilicia in southern Asia Minor.*

Cyrene. *A port city in Libya famous for its trade. It was founded in the seventh century B.C. by colonists from the island of Thera. Cretans also settled there.*

Cyrus. *Founder of the Persian Empire.*

Danaids. *Fifty Greek sisters who, with the exception of one, murdered their Egyptian husbands at their father's (Danaus') command. The forty-nine were punished in Hades by having to try to fill leaky jars with water.*

Delia. *The first love of Tibullus, who apparently was of plebeian extraction. We are told by Apuleius that her real name was Plania.*

Delos. *An island in the Aegean Sea on which Apollo and Diana were born. It was a center for the worship of Apollo.*

Delphi. *A Greek city in Phocis situated on the southern slopes of Mt. Parnassus; famous for its temple and oracle of Apollo.*

Diana. *Sister of Apollo, who had various spheres of activity. She is the moon-goddess, goddess of the hunt, and a patron goddess of women in labor; the Greek Artemis.*

Dictynna. *An epithet given to Diana but properly belonging to the Cretan goddess Britomartis, with whom she is often identified. In her attempt to escape from Minos, Britomartis leaped over a cliff into the sea and was caught in fishermen's nets (Greek* diktyon *= net).*

Dionysus. *Identical with Bacchus, god of wine.*

Dogstar. *The bright star Sirius in the constellation of Canis Major; always associated by the ancients with intense summer heat.*

Don. *A river over a thousand miles long in Russia which flows into the Sea of Azov.*

Elysian Fields. *The abode of the blest in the Lower World.*

Erigone. *The daughter of the legendary Athenian Icarius. (See note 93.)*

Falernum. *An area of Campania in southern Italy; famous for its wine.*

Fates. *The three Fates (Lat.* Parcae*) wove the web of every man's life. Lachesis assigns each man's lot, Klotho actually spins the thread of life, and Atropos cuts it. The Latin names are Nona, Decuma, and Morta.*

Gauls. *A Celtic tribe from France with which the Romans often had to contend.*

Gyndes. *A tributary of the Tigris river in Persia; now the Diala or Kerkah.*

Hecate. *A goddess associated with sorcery and black magic who was wor-*

shipped at the cross-roads; often considered the goddess of the mysterious moon. She was accompanied by dogs, no doubt because of the effect of moonlight on these animals. Hecate was often identified with Diana.

Helvetia. *The ancient country corresponding roughly to Switzerland.*

Hercules. *Son of Jupiter and Alcmena, celebrated for his strength and for the twelve labors imposed upon him as a result of Juno's hatred.*

Herophyle. *A Trojan Sibyl born at Marpessos not far from Troy, but often claimed by Erythrae, a city in Ionia. (See* Sibyl.)

Hirtius. *Aulus Hirtius, one of the consuls for the year 43 B.C., died in battle in the same year.*

Hyperion. *Son of a Titan and the Earth and father of the Sun. (See* Titan.)

Iapydia. *A section of northern Illyria (roughly modern Yugoslavia) inhabited by barbaric peoples who were subjugated after they revolted in 36 B.C.*

Icarius. *A legendary Athenian who once entertained Bacchus and as a result learned the art of making wine. (See note 93.)*

Ilia. *The poetic name for Rhea Silvia, daughter of Numitor and mother of Romulus and Remus by Mars.*

Isis. *An Egyptian goddess of fertility; sister and wife of the god Osiris. (See* Osiris.)

Ithaca. *The island kingdom of Ulysses in the Ionian Sea.*

Ixion. *A mortal who tried to seduce Juno. He was punished by Jupiter by being bound to a continuously revolving wheel in Hades.*

Jove. *Identical with Jupiter, king of the gods.*

Juno. *Wife and sister of Jupiter and Queen of the gods; the Greek Hera.*

Jupiter. *King of the gods; the Greek Zeus.*

Laconia. *The southeastern district of the Peloponnese, whose principal city was Sparta.*

Laestrygonia. *A mythical country of cannibals in the* Odyssey *ruled by Antiphates. Attempts have been made to identify the place with the area around Formiae in Campania.*

Lares. *The Lares (singular, Lar) were the tutelar deities of a Roman family. Together with the Penates they constituted the household gods.*

Latona. *Mother of Apollo and Diana; the Greek Leto.*

Laurentum. *A settlement on the left bank of the Tiber river in Latium, founded by Aeneas and his followers.*

Lavinium. *A town near the sea coast in Latium not far from Rome, founded by Aeneas after he married Lavinia, daughter of King Latinus; now Pratica di Mare. (See* Turnus.)

Lenaeus. *Another name for Bacchus, god of wine.*

Lethe. *The river of forgetfulness in the Lower World.*

Lucina. *An epithet of the goddess Juno. (See note 71.)*

Lydia. *A country in western Asia Minor; noted for its natural wealth.*

Lygdamus. *Author of the elegies in Book III of the* Corpus Tibullianum. *Attempts have been made to identify him with Propertius, Ovid, and Ovid's brother, none of which are convincing. He writes of his love for Neaera, from whom he is estranged.*

Macer. *A friend of Tibullus; possibly to be identified with the poet Aemilius Macer.*

Maera. *The dog of the Athenian Icarius. (See* Icarius *and note 93.)*

Marathus. *A lad with whom Tibullus may have had an affair.*

Marcia. *The praetor Quintus Marcius Rex built an aqueduct in 144 B.C. The water which it supplied, famous for its purity, was known as the* aqua Marcia.

Mars. *God of war; the Greek Ares.*

Medea. *Princess of Colchis who helped Jason obtain the Golden Fleece through her powers of witchcraft.*

Melampus. *Son of Amythaon and celebrated prophet and missionary of Bacchus.*

Messalla. *M. Valerius Messalla Corvinus, the statesman, orator, general, and patron of literature. Tibullus was the luminary of his literary circle.*

Messalinus. *M. Valerius Messalla Messalinus was the eldest son of Messalla, Tibullus' literary patron. The fifth poem of Book II was written upon the occasion of his election to the board of* quindecemviri *(fifteen men who had charge of certain religious matters).*

Minerva. *Goddess of wisdom; the Greek Athena.*

Minos. *King of Crete and father of Ariadne. He built the famous Labyrinth at Knossos which held the Minotaur.*

Molorchus. *A poor vineyard keeper at Cleonae. (See note 94.)*

Muses. *A group of nine goddesses who presided over literature and the arts and sciences.*

Naiad. *The name given to any nymph inhabiting a fountain or spring.*

Neaera. *The loved one of Lygdamus, author of Book III of the* Corpus Tibullianum.

Nemesis. *The name of Tibullus' second love, treated in Book II; undoubtedly a pseudonym.*

Neptune. *Brother of Jupiter and god of the sea; the Greek Poseidon.*

Nestor. *King of Pylos in the western Peloponnese, who took part in the expedition against Troy. He lived over a hundred years and was famous for his wisdom and eloquence.*

Nisus. *A king of Megara. (See note 14.)*

Numicus. *Apparently once a small river, but now to be identified with the tiny stream known as the Rio Torto. It was located near Lavinium. Aeneas died near the river and was worshipped as the patron deity of the immediate area.*

Olympus. *A mountain almost 10,000 feet high on the borders of Macedonia and Thessaly; home of the gods.*

Oroatis. *A river in the Persian province of Susiana flowing into the Persian Gulf.*

Osiris. *An Egyptian god of fertility who was worshipped along with Isis, his sister and wife. Their cult involved a complicated ritual. In Egypt Osiris was generally considered the god of the Underworld.*

Paedeans. *A cannibalistic tribe in India.*

Palatine. *One of the seven hills of Rome. In imperial times the Roman emperor resided there.*

Pales. *A patron goddess of shepherds and cattle.*

Pan. *Greco-Roman god of the woods and of shepherds.*

Pansa. *Gaius Vibius Pansa, one of the consuls for the year 43 B.C., died in battle in the same year.*

Pelops. *Son of Tantalus and grandfather of Agamemnon and Menelaus. In his childhood his father served him as food for the gods. Jupiter restored him to life and substituted an ivory shoulder for the one eaten by Ceres.*

Pentheus. *Grandson of Cadmus and king of Thebes; for his death, see note 86.*

Persephone. *In Greek mythology the daughter of Demeter, the earth-mother goddess. Hades took her by force to the Lower World, where she is his queen for one-third of the year. She spends the remainder of the year with her mother on earth; the Roman Proserpine.*

Phaeacia. *That is, Corcyra, with which Scheria, the land of the Phaeacians in Homer, is identified.*

Phoebus. *Identical with Apollo. (See* Apollo.)

Phoenicia. *A country of Syria famous for its trade and purple dyes.*

Pholoe. *A young girl with whom Marathus has fallen in love in the eighth poem of Book I.*

Phrygia. *A territory comprising the western and central area of Asia Minor. Like Lydia it was famous for its natural wealth. Troy was located there.*

Phryne. *The name of Nemesis' bawdy social secretary. A famous Athenian semi-prostitute had the same name.*

Phyto. *The Sibyl of Samos. (See* Sibyl.)

Pieria. *A country in Macedonia where the Muses were born. They are often called the* Pierides.

Pluto. *Brother of Jupiter and Neptune and king of the Lower World; the Greek Hades.*

Priapus. *Son of Bacchus and god of fertility in general. He was the patron god of gardens and vineyards.*

Pylos. *A very old city on the shore of the western Peloponnese; home of Nestor. (See* Nestor.)

Romulus. *Son of Rhea Silvia and Mars and brother of Remus; legendary founder and first king of Rome.*

Rufus Valgius. *A member of the poetic circle of Maecenas and friend of Horace; writer of epic verse, none of which has survived.*

Rutulians. *An indigenous people of Latium ruled by Turnus. Aeneas and his followers fought with them for supremacy.*

Samos. *An island off the coast of Asia Minor famous for its pottery.*

Saturn. *Father of Jupiter. During the Golden Age he was king of the gods. Jupiter finally wrested power from him; the Greek Kronos.*

Scylla. *A monster with dogs growing out of her loins who lived in a cave on the Italian shore of the Straits of Messina and who ate sailors who sailed by. The maelstrom Charybdis faced opposite her, and passing through the channel between the two meant certain death.*

Scythia. *The name given by the Romans to the large area between the Carpathian mountains and the river Don. The indigenous tribes were noted for their barbarism.*

Servius. *The father of the poetess Sulpicia.*

Sibyl. *Properly the name of a single female soothsayer who was variously localized. Actually there were probably several prophetesses by this name, all of whom were associated with the worship of Apollo. The most famous is the Sibyl at Cumae in the time of Aeneas. The Sibyl's prophecies were recorded in the Sibylline books and were frequently consulted.*

Sidon. *A very ancient city in Phoenicia and mother city of Tyre; famous for its purple dyes.*

Sirens. *Enchantresses, half bird and half woman, who lured men to their death through their song. (See note 104.)*

Sulpicia. *The ward of Messalla and member of his literary circle. In Book IV of the* Corpus Tibullianum *she writes of her love for Cerinthus.*

Syrtis. *The shallow water off the northern coast of Africa. Stories to the effect that it was hazardous for sailors were common.*

Tamyris. *A queen of the Massagetae in northern Asia Minor. She defeated and killed Cyrus I of Persia.*

Tantalus. *An immortal who, having been admitted to a banquet of the gods, stole their food and gave it to mortals. He was punished in Hades by being forever hungry and thirsty. He stands in water up to his chin, but when he tries to drink, the water disappears. Similarly, when he tries to reach the fruit which hangs over his head, a wind blows it away.*

Taurus. *A high mountain range in Cilicia in southeastern Asia Minor; now Bulghar Dagh.*

Thessaly. *A country in northern Greece; frequently considered a land of marvels and black magic.*

Thetis. *A sea nymph to whom it was prophesied that she would give birth to a son mightier than his father. She married the mortal Peleus and gave birth to the hero Achilles.*

Thrace. *The eastern half of the Balkan peninsula north of Macedonia.*

Tisiphone. *One of the furies or spirits who punished the doers of unavenged crimes. They tormented the wicked in Hades.*

Titan. *The name given to any of the older gods who preceded the Olympians.*

Titius. *A man mentioned in the fourth poem of Book I; his identity is not certain. (See note 17.)*

Tityos. *A giant who was punished in Hades for his attempt to seduce Leto. He was stretched over nine acres and a vulture fed on his liver, which was constantly reproduced.*

Troy. *The capitol of Priam's Phrygian kingdom, destroyed in the Trojan War.*

Turnus. *King of the Rutulians, an indigenous people in Latium with whom Aeneas and his Trojan band fought for supremacy. Turnus had been betrothed to Lavinia, daughter of Latinus, king of the Latins. The engagement was broken and Lavinia was then promised to Aeneas. Turnus was killed in battle by Aeneas, who married Lavinia and founded the town of Lavinium.*

Tuscany. *The modern name for Tuscia or Etruria, the area of central Italy between Rome and Florence inhabited by the Etruscans.*

Tusculum. *A city in Italy located approximately fifteen miles southeast of Rome; close to the modern Frascati.*

Tyre. *An important commercial city on the coast of Phoenicia, famous for its purple dyes.*

Ulysses. *King of Ithaca, famous among the Greek heroes of the Trojan War for his cunning and eloquence. After the fall of Troy he wandered for many years before he reached home.*

Vesta. *Daughter of Saturn and virgin goddess of the hearth and of flocks and herds.*

Vestals. *Virgin priestesses of the goddess Vesta.*